Aerial of St. Mary's Home campus — 1952

A Test of Time

History of St. Mary's Home
1889 – 1989

by
Wilfred P. Schoenberg, S.J.

Foreword by
Emma Dennis

Research Assistant
Adam Heineman

Cover designed by
Danielle Tanner and Tracy Yates

Editors: Emma Dennis and Adam Heineman

Graphic Design: Tracy Yates

Typesetting: Debra Mecartea

Printing: PrintGraphics, Beaverton, Oregon

Binding: Lincoln and Allen, Portland, Oregon

Published by:
St. Mary's Home for Boys
16535 S.W. Tualatin Valley Hwy.
Beaverton, Oregon 97006

ISBN: 0-9625179-0-9

Copyright ©1989 St. Mary's Home for Boys

All rights reserved. No part of this publication may be reproduced, stored in a retrieval system, or transmitted in any form or by any means, electronic, mechanical, photocopying, recording, or otherwise, without the prior permission of the copyright owner, except for brief quotations included in a review of the book.

*This book is dedicated to a
"special group" of religious and lay men and women
for their dedication, sacrifice and love of children.
The Staff of St. Mary's Home, 1889 – 1989.*

Table of Contents

Acknowledgments..x
Foreword xii
Chapter 1 The Beginnings 1
Chapter 2 The Early Years 21
Chapter 3 The Years of Peaceful Survival 45
Chapter 4 The Golden Age Continued 59
Chapter 5 The War Years and After 83
Chapter 6 Change of the Guard 99
Chapter 7 The Painful Transition.................117
Chapter 8 A Treatment Center.....................135
Chapter 9 The Recent Years 159
Epilogue 181
Notes..183

Acknowledgments

There are two pleasant experiences in the composition of a book. The first is completing it. The second is having an opportunity to express publicly one's appreciation to those who have helped to make it possible. The latter are too many to list, but I wish to recall those whose contributions should not go unrecognized.

Three especially should be mentioned: Emma Dennis the Executive Director of St. Mary's Home for Boys, who invited me to compose this centenary history; Dr. Loyal Marsh, Associate Director, who gave me generously of his time; and, Adam Heineman, an enthusiastic alumnus, who has run down many obscure leads and gathered valuable data.

Two others among the alumni should be mentioned: Mike Cole, whose all morning interview provided solid evidence for many judgements made, and countless little details to boot; and, Richard Hansen, who shared his personal memoirs.

The cooperation of several archivists has been long suffering as well as cheerful: Mary Grant, Archivist for the Archdiocese of Portland in Oregon; Sister Rosemarie Kasper, S.N.J.M., Archivist for the Sisters of the Holy Names, of Jesus and Mary, Marylhurst; Sister Mary Charlene, S.S.M.O., Archivist for the Sisters of St. Mary of Oregon, Beaverton; Father Milton Ballor, C.PP.S., Archivist for the Society of the Precious Blood in Carthagena, Ohio; and Father Neill Meany, S.J., Archivist for the Oregon Province of the Society of Jesus in Spokane.

Others to whom I turned for help were Sister Anna Hertel, S.S.M.O., Superior General of the Sisters of St. Mary of Oregon, who graciously gave permission for the use of copyrighted material; Sister Mary Andre Lafferty, O.S.F., Superior General of the Franciscan Missionary Sisters, who placed at my disposal no small amount of valued material; and Sister Mary Fidelis Kreutzer, S.S.M.O., to whom I am always indebted.

Finally, my special thanks to my Provincial, Father Frank Case, S.J., for allowing me time to undertake this welcome task; our Province Treasurer, Father Edward Favilla, S.J. for supporting me; Father Leo Kaufmann, S.J., for reading and correcting the typescript; Terri Steen, the happy receptionist at St. Mary's, who helped in various ways; Devin Recci, who identified buildings on the campus, on a sunny spring day; Mr. William P. Sherman, whose assistance has always been indispensable; and my tolerant and sweet little typist Charis Sherman Howser, who has always gone far beyond the call of duty to meet sometimes impossible deadlines.

If I have missed others, my apologies. Blame it on the midnight hour when one's energies are low and one's wits are shattered.

WPS

Foreword

As we celebrate the 100th birthday of a person, a nation, or even a charitable agency, it is only right and proper that we reminisce about past times and events and not only record those historical happenings for today's generation, but also for the sake of posterity.

In reading "A Test of Time," we must remove the veil of political, social, and personal struggles and incompetencies. We must see God's hand molding and using every mysterious happening for His purpose. We must admire the strength and perseverance of the dedicated staff, who endured great hardship, and who happily sacrificed personal wants for the love of children. Lastly, we think about the thousands of children who needed and received help. We realize that the importance of children must never be slighted and our investments in them must never waiver.

We are indebted and grateful to Reverend Wilfred Shoenberg, S.J., a highly skilled and qualified historian, for telling this story, and to Reverend Frank Case, S.J., Provincial of the Oregon Province, for allowing this to become a reality.

Emma Dennis
Executive Director
1989

Chapter 1

The Beginnings

Oregon's first Archbishop was a stern man. Age did little to mellow him, though it must be admitted he was more approachable in his late seventies than he was when he came to Oregon in 1838. His name was Francis Norbert Blanchet. One had to be careful to remember his first name because he had a brother who was also a Bishop, across the river at Vancouver, Washington Territory. Both had come from eastern Canada, where an immense flock of Blanchets, all related by blood, was noted for its devotion to the Church.

Francis Norbert was generally regarded as "holy," but he was also bossy and stubborn. His subjects saw in him, however, one little characteristic which they liked: his ready concern for sick or homeless children. This endeared him to all. His heart may have been a little too rigid, but at least it was in the right place.

Unfortunately, His Excellency had been unable to establish what was called in those days "an orphanage," at least one with a name over the door like "Holy Angels" or "St. Joseph's" or something else properly pious. There was one orphanage across the river at Vancouver, where the Sisters of Providence had a saintly nun who ran it along with a lot of other holy places like academies and hospitals. Her name was Mother Joseph of the Sacred Heart. She loved orphan children and she was not above bribing them with chocolate to say their prayers. Her statue is now in the National Hall of Fame in Washington, D.C.[1]

2 A TEST OF TIME

All Prelates photos courtesy of Historical Archives, Archdiocese of Portland in Oregon

Archbishop Francis Norbert Blanchet — purchased in 1861 640 acres which later became the site of St. Mary's Home.

Archbishop Blanchet was like her in this respect: he treated children, whenever he met them at the hospital or Sisters' school, with cookies and candies. Years before, when he was a young missionary with the Indians, he used cookies to reward them. None but the Indians were aware of this and His Excellency said little about it. Perhaps he feared the worst, that he would be accused of making "rice Christians."

On the Portland side of the river, twelve Sisters of the Holy Names of Jesus and Mary from eastern Canada, established an academy in 1859. Local big wigs were very proud of having in their city, which they regarded as the "Boston of the West," a convent school where young ladies could be prepared for genteel wifely and motherly careers. While these goals were doubtlessly intended by the Sisters, when they came here, they had in mind other children who were less fortunate. The Sisters seldom had to advertise for them.

The First Orphanage at St. Mary's in Portland

In the convent *Chronicle* of Villa Marie one of the Sisters modestly recorded the following:

> The Catholic Church in Oregon as early as 1859 directed its attention to caring for the orphan, without regard for creed. When in that year the Sisters of the Holy Names of Jesus and Mary had laid the foundations of Catholic educational work by establishing St. Mary's Academy; it seemed an admitted fact that the parentless girl without means should receive from the Sisters the same kindly solicitude as bestowed upon the student whose parents met the prescribed rates. Many of the pioneer students of St. Mary's were daughters of influential and cultured families . . . . Be it said to the honor of these noble hearted girls that they not only shared in the privations of the Sisters, but became their auxiliaries in caring for homeless little girls who were the wards of the academy.[2]

This, then, was the formal beginning of Catholic care of orphans in the "Boston-of-the-West." The Sisters took the initiative and until the Archdiocese was better placed to take over this care, the Sisters continued it at their own expense for three long decades.

During this time they did not neglect the boys. The unidentified Sister in her *Chronicle* continued:

> A boarding and day school for boys [was] opened by the Sisters of the Holy Names on November 20, 1859. That which St. Mary's had been to the friendless girls, St. Joseph's became to the orphan boys. The two schools continued in their work under the above described conditions until 1871, when the Most Reverend Francis N. Blanchet laid the foundation of St. Michael's College under the direction of the Reverend A.J. Glorieux [later] Bishop of Boise. This new school naturally relieved the Sisters of the duty of teaching boys. The building on Twelfth [sic] and Mill was converted into a home for girls under the title of St. Joseph's Orphanage.[3] At the close of the scholastic year 1871-1872, the records showed that sixty girls found an asylum under the hospitable roof of the new institution. The funds for the maintenance of these children came from the treasury of St. Mary's Academy. Through the seventies and eighties the Sisters kept up this work of caring for orphan girls.[4]

There are no records on how many boys were taken in between 1859 and 1871. Frequent entries with reference to arrivals, however, appear in the *Chronicle* of St. Mary's Academy.

> *November 11, 1861. Another orphan. A poor woman appeals to us to accept one of her little boys as she has no means of supporting him.*
>
> *December 24, 1862. Our dear Infant Jesus asks an act of charity from us in the form of two little boys, age respectively seven and two and one half years who were left on our grounds at five o'clock this evening. The poor little ones, sadly neglected, begged us to receive them.*
>
> *January 12, 1863. A little boy aged eight years, found in our grounds, was brought to us by a young man, who begged us to give him an asylum. No one can give any information about the child's parents.*
>
> *And two months later.*
>
> *March 7, 1863. Two little orphans, William and Marshall, aged seven and five . . . .*[5]

For adults who have enjoyed having warm, loving homes all of their lives it is difficult to imagine the fear and loneliness in the hearts of these little boys. Abandoned by the only ones they ever knew, cold and hungry in a strange place, they evoked a generous response in the Sisters, one of whom had this to say about it. "Had no other reward than the happy faces of those homeless children on being introduced to their surroundings, this would have proved an ample reward . . . ."

The Foundlings

Even more tragic are references to foundlings in the Sisters' *Chronicle*. Only two appear here to reveal not only the gentle kindness of the Sisters, but also the risks they took in performing these acts of charity.

> *September 15, 1866. Sister Mary Isidore on going to open the gate this morning found a little infant a few days old lying in the garden. Its only dress was a piece of old blanket that partly covered its tiny body. It had evidently been thrown over the fence for one side of its face was badly bruised. It is an established regulation that a Sister shall never be alone in taking in one of these waifs. This is a measure of good prudence as we live in a Protestant country and we can not be too careful in exposing ourselves to slander. Besides, should legal troubles*

ensue, a witness would be required. Lucien Bourgault generally enjoyed the honorable function of rescuing these little waifs. The first act of charity for these little ones was the bath and the providing them with suitable clothing. Baptism was then administered to the little waif by Reverend Father Piette. The name of Mary Margaret was given her. Her sponsors were Mr. McKay and Mrs. O'Brien. The significant surname of De Rachat (redeemed) was given her. She is to be cared for by a woman who devotes herself to the raising of these foundlings.[6]

This "little waif" died on November 7. Others soon replaced it. On "October 19, 1867. The holy angels brought us a little candidate for baptism. Like her predecessors, this foundling scarcely three days old, is rescued from the front garden by Lucien Bourgault, and like them, after going through the routine of soap, water and dressing, she is baptized . . . Lucien acting as sponsor. She is confided to Mrs. O'Brien."

These foundlings, if they lived, were turned over to "reliable foster parents" until they were old enough for schooling. Meanwhile, the Sisters paid ten dollars per month to the foster parents, like Mrs. O'Brien, for each baby's care. The cost was a real hardship on the Sisters, but they never faltered in their care of orphans.

The Land

Archbishop Blanchet, meanwhile, was not oblivious to these charitable activities. By a series of quitclaim deeds, dated as early as August 28, 1861, he obtained title to land about ten miles west of Portland, in an area now generally called Beaverton. This title was contingent upon certain developments, most notably, confirmation by the government of the original land claim. On June 24, 1865, the conveyances to Blanchet were "perfected" by the recording of a Donation Land Claim for the widow and heir of John Elliott, "who was the original owner of the property." This document was signed by President Andrew Johnson, Abraham Lincoln's successor in the White House.[7]

So the Archbishop had land, some six hundred acres of it. But lacking other resources the land lay idle beneath the Oregon skies, and the trees grew taller, and the bushes thicker, and to the north, the broad swamp got soggier. It was an area so heavy with foliage that one could get lost in it only a hundred feet from the trail. In other words, it was a potentially dangerous wilderness within a much vaster wilderness, covering hundreds of square miles.

This is what the Archbishop acquired in 1861.

The New Archbishop

In 1880, Blanchet resigned at the venerable age of eighty-five. He was succeeded by Bishop Charles Seghers of the Diocese of Vancouver Island in British Columbia. Seghers was regarded as an uncommonly holy man, but he was stubborn too. He had come from Belgium as a young priest and he loved nothing more than traveling to remote places to preach about Jesus Christ and His good news. He lasted as Archbishop of Oregon City less than five years, and most of this time he was exploring the outer reaches of his Archdiocese to let the people know that the Church was interested in them. Then, with the reluctant approval of Pope Leo XIII, he resigned his see and returned to Vancouver Island as Bishop, partly because the priest whom the Pope appointed did not want to be a Bishop, and partly because Seghers wanted to keep a promise he had made.

At that time, the mission of Alaska was attached to the Diocese of Vancouver Island. Seghers had gone there on several occasions and on his last voyage to the interior had promised the natives that he would return to build a Church. So, after resigning his position as Archbishop, he returned in the summer of 1886. In central Alaska, in a fish camp on the Yukon River, he was murdered. It was a frigid, early morning on November 26 and he was within a day's journey of his goal. The man who killed him was his own companion on that terrible trail across Chilkoot Pass and down the frigid lonely river.[8]

Archbishop Seghers had never got around to building an orphanage for Portland's homeless children. When he left for Alaska, it was said, the children in the Sisters' homes shed tears. This is not surprising, since for many of them, tears had often been their only bread. The Archbishop, too, was very sad to leave them, but his restless heart was already beating with the excitement that lay ahead.

Archbishop William Gross, Founder

William Gross, previously Bishop of Savannah, Georgia, became the third Archbishop of Oregon City. A native of Baltimore, where the Church had been established for one hundred and fifty years, Gross was a member of the Congregation of the Holy Redeemer (the Redemptorists) and was an old friend of Cardinal James Gibbons, the most influential prelate in contemporary America. Gibbons had lost his own father when he was a mere boy. This and other circumstances of his life helped to form him as a special friend of the poor, the hungry and the homeless. In these respects, Gross was like him. As Bishop of Savannah, he had built a large orphanage there, and if the truth were known, he was not happy to leave it behind. It is not surprising then that one of his first projects in Oregon was to build an orphanage.

Gross arrived in Portland on May 23, 1885, to see what the Holy Father had given him in place of Savannah. We know what he expected because he wrote a letter about it.[9] He had expected an impoverished flock and a primitive city. What he found instead, when he stepped off the boat, which had carried him down the Columbia and up the Willamette, was a throng of prosperous looking people gathered around a huge arch of flowers to give him a noisy welcome. St. Michael's College band, little fellows with big lungs, could be heard above the happy clatter and when the initial formalities ended, the band led the long procession to the Cathedral. The Archbishop, following at the tail of it, could see in the evening twilight the heavily wooded hills to the west. Before him, blocking his vision in some places, were many multi-storied buildings and elegant homes. No one had told him that Portland was the "Boston of the West."

The Province (or Archdiocese) of Oregon City, when Gross came to direct it, consisted of three dioceses, Oregon City, Nesqually and Helena, and one vicariate, Idaho.[10] The jurisdiction of the Archbishop was restricted mostly to Oregon, a state as large as Maryland and New York combined, with most of the New England states thrown in for good measure. There were only twenty-nine priests in the whole Archdiocese, including four Benedictines, who were subject to the Archbishop only in certain matters. The area was more than enough for Gross. He tended to be monkish, a prelate of scholarly rather than of an activity temperament. He much preferred to do things quietly, using a catspaw if he could, and he usually took his time for making a decision. It was almost four years before a brick was laid to hold up a flimsy frame building, pretensiously called an orphanage.

Archbishop William Gross, C.Ss.R. — soon after his arrival one of his top priorities was to establish a Catholic home for orphans.

First Step: The Sisters

Although His Excellency had recognized the need for an orphanage from the beginning, he was unable to provide it, or even think about it, for some months. Due to the long absences of his predecessor, the Archdiocese was in a state something like suspended animation. Thus he had to resolve countless crises, among which was the unfinished new cathedral on Third and Stark.

Another, which had been called to his attention by the busy monks at Mount Angel, was a colony of stiff-necked Catholics, who had come recently from Minnesota in very peculiar circumstances. They had settled in the foothills of the Cascades near a one horse town called Jordan. Lacking a priest, this colony was ruled like a theocracy by three lay trustees, who acted more like despots than Christian leaders.

Reportedly, some nuns were living there, also, in a two-room hut, trying to survive as religious without spiritual direction or the sacraments.

The Archbishop had reason to be alarmed. The Sisters, he was told, were being held there virtually as prisoners by their own parents. There was some irregularity about their status in the Church, about which they knew nothing. Near their "convent" was the shrine of a priest, whose long dead corpse had been brought from Minnesota to be venerated as the relics of a saint.

The Sisters regarded themselves as members of the Society of the Most Precious Blood. Their fate had carried them from Ohio to Minnesota to Oregon, and now, there they were, pious as Church mice and eager to serve God as religious in the Catholic Church.

His Excellency needed no prodding. He knew an opportunity when he saw one. He could use an order of Sisters to help with his schools, and especially to staff an orphanage. He agreed to meet with members of the colony on July 31, 1885, a little over two months after his arrival in Portland.

The Crisis at Jordan

The trip to Jordan was long and tedious. His Excellency occupied a seat on the Toonerville train to Scio, then another seat in Father Werner's buggy which bumped along a primitive road to the little Church on the hillside. Nearby, conspicuously standing out, like a monsignor among priests, the shrine of Father Joseph Albrecht, caught his eye. What he thought about it is not hard to guess. He found the trustees respectful, even joyful, and the rest of the people in a holiday mood, carrying banners and singing songs of welcome. He offered holy Mass in the Church, conferred the sacrament of Confirmation on many, then laid down the law, the shrine had to go. The deed to the Church property had to be transferred to the Archbishop. The trustees had to subject themselves to Church authority in matters concerning the Church.

As for the Sisters, the Archbishop told them plainly what they must do. He spoke to them in German.

As he talked to them, he was impressed by their faith, sincerity and evident good will. At last he asked the group if they would like to join him in his apostolic work, and received a spontaneous pledge to do everything in their power to assist him. They grieved that they had so little to offer. He promised to send a teacher to train them in the religious life which was, of necessity, the first step toward this end. Then Sister Lucretia rose and kneeling at the feet of His Excellency assured him that they would do whatever was necessary to correct their position in the Church. It was a very satisfactory beginning and Archbishop Gross was well satisfied. "You will be my Sisters and help me in my work," he told them. The Archbishop commissioned Father Werner to start a course of instructions to prepare the young women for religious profession of vows. There was great joy in the convent.[11]

Before the storm occasioned by some of the Archbishop's demands broke over the heads of the colonists, the Archbishop departed quietly for Portland.

Eventually the prior of Mount Angel, Father Adelhelm Odermatt, accompanied by Father Werner Ruttiman, visited Jordan twice as emissaries of the Archbishop. Werner had discovered the plight of the Sisters in the first place and until his untimely death he would be their staunchest support.

After the Sisters had gathered together, Adelhelm presented them with a statement which had been composed in the Chancery, a declaration of allegiance to the Church and of determination to sever all connections with the trustees of Jordan. Each Sister was asked to consider the document well and to sign it only if free and willing to do so. Each one signed it. They were as follows: Superior Lucretia [Hauck], blind Afra Ruhl, Theresa Arnold, Emma Bleily, Mary Ann Foltz, Aurelia Boedigheimer, Martha Eifert, Elizabeth Eifert, Theresa Foltz, Catherine Eifert, Elizabeth Foltz, Erana Reisterer, Matilda Silbernagel, Mary Barbara Silbernagel, Anna Bender, and Elizabeth Bender. Seven of those who signed were daughters of trustees.

The trustees were then summoned. They arrived in good humor, smiling pleasantly and nodding to the two Benedictines. But when Adelhelm read the Archbishop's letter and informed them of what the Sisters had done, they were thunderstruck. Adelhelm took advantage of their silence. He requested each Sister, who sincerely desired to accept the Archbishop's proposal, to stand. "They rose as a single body and stood straight and tall." The trustees were smiling no longer.

Maria Zell Convent

Eight of the Sisters left Jordan on Saturday, June 12, 1886, in two farm wagons provided by Father Werner. Surrounded by their frugal possessions and sitting on boxes as improvised benches, they looked back to see the only relatives and friends they had ever known, standing on the hillside near the little Church. Some were weeping and the Sisters wept, too, as the wagons jerkily pulled away.[12]

Werner took them to the Benedictine Sisters' Convent at Gervais, Oregon, in Mount Angel's overlook, which covered something like ninety square miles on a clear day. There they remained for two months, cooking, sewing, washing laundry, praying — and hoping. The Benedictines wanted to make Benedictine nuns out of them, but they resisted vigorously, saying that they were the Archbishop's Sisters. They wanted to know when the Archbishop would provide them with their own convent. Had he abandoned them? Father Werner said "no" and told them that he would go to Portland to see the Archbishop. When he did, His Excellency assured Werner of his support "for the nine young ladies" as he liked to call them. He also offered them a choice of two sites for their new convent.

The first was in Milwaukie, a village south of Portland, where a little mission Church had been built some two decades earlier. It was called St. John's, and a priest came there from Portland periodically, to confer the sacraments and to offer Mass. The second choice was Sublimity, where Father Werner conducted services in a ramshackle old building, a former United Brethren College. The Sisters, if they chose to do so, could live on the second floor, but of course they would have to repaint it. The windows were broken and bats and swallows flitted in and out with a rush of air and a noise like a boomerang. The floor sagged, the stairway needed replacing. There were no furnishings.

If the Sisters had any doubts, the presence of Werner resolved them. They had learned to trust him, and despite his grumpy and sometimes bossy ways, like many priests, they had come to love him as a holy and compassionate monk.

They informed the Archbishop of their choice and on August 14, 1886, two of the Sisters, Emma Bleily and Catherine Eifert, moved into the dilapidated ruin, which Werner had named, without consulting them, "Maria Zell Convent." For him the title was reminiscent of a favored Marian shrine in Austria.

On the day following this ecstatic occupation, the feast of the Assumption of Mary, Werner offered Mass in the first floor "temporary" Church. The two Sisters, overdressed like some statues of the Infant of Prague, almost buried under many yards of black cloth, and bearing up bravely with heavy crucifixes around their necks, attended the service piously, scarcely recognizing the historic nature of the event.

For many years since, it has been regarded as the birthday of Oregon's Sisters of St. Mary.

The First Proposal For An Orphanage

In mid-winter of 1887, the time had come for the Sisters' vows. There were ten Sisters now, because a local girl, Mary Giebler by name, had joined them as their "holy innocent." In keeping with contemporary customs, they decided to choose new names for religious life.

> .... The results were as follows: Barbara Hauck, known as Sister Lucretia, decided to change her religious name to Sister Mary Clara; Theresa Arnold, who had been deeply impressed at Mount Angel, took Sister Mary Benedict; Emma (Emerentiana) Bleily, "wishing to have the same heavenly protector as His Excellency," became Sister Mary Wilhelmina; Catherine Eiffert chose Sister Mary Josephine; Aurelia Boedigheimer became Sister Mary Cecelia; Mary Silbernagel "chose the name of the beautiful mystic St. Gertrude," becoming Sister Mary Gertrude; Anna Bender "loved St. Aloysius who had dared the anger of his father to follow his vocation, and she wished for the name of Sister Mary Aloysius;" Martha Eiffert took Sister Mary Rose "in honor of the humble little virgin of Lima;" Matilda Silbernagel took the saint of her birthday, December 27, and became Sister Mary Johana; and the youngest of all, referred to as "the holy innocent," wanted "a great penitent for her patroness and became Sister Mary Magdalene."[13]

The weather was very cold that winter and the snow was deep. Spring had arrived, however, when the Archbishop arrived at Maria Zell on March 24 to preside over the ceremony of the vows. He summoned the Sisters to inform them regarding his plans for their future in the Archdiocese. One of his gravest obligations, he said, was the establishment of an orphanage for the archdiocese. At present, destitute children were being placed in non-Catholic institutions where they received no Catholic instructions whatever. He was making preparations for a new building to house these children and it was his intention to place them under the care of this new congregation.

Also, His Excellency added, new parochial schools were soon to be erected in many parishes. The Sisters were to begin immediately to prepare themselves to direct Catholic education in them. To start with, they were to organize classes in Christian Doctrine in the Sublimity parish. There was great need for training the children close at hand. The Church had been neglected in this district, and a strong Catholic laity would be its hope for the future. The parish had been without a resident priest until the Benedictine Fathers had come and the people by that time had become too involved in seeking material wealth. The Sisters could change this by instructing the children.[14]

On the following day, March 25, 1887, the five older Sisters pronounced their vows of poverty, chastity and obedience. The five who were younger were formally clothed in the habits of novices. All ten, with gentle admonitions from the prelate, began the long critical period of preparation for their appointed roles as teachers and step mothers for countless children as yet unborn.

The First Begging Tour

During the months that followed, not all was rosy and serene at Maria Zell. Sister Wilhelmina had been elected as superior, which is to say she now directed a penniless institution, a convent of otherworldly nuns, most of whom did not know enough English to attend local schools. "You have Father Werner to advise you," was the Archbishop's parting benediction, as though Werner could wave a wand and fill the shelves with food. "There is no way," His Excellency had added dryly, "to relieve the present situation without going out to beg."

So Wilhelmina went out to beg. She chose for her companion Sister Cecelia, whose father Bruno Boedingheimer donated $100 for travel expenses. She also accepted free passage for herself and Cecelia on the Northern Pacific Railway, which Father Werner had arranged. On a cheerless Friday in mid-summer, 1888, the two Sisters, looking hot and forlorn in their long, black habits, like two bewildered pilgrims, boarded an evening train in Portland and rolled off into the twilight.

The Begging Tour eventually became renowned in the community's history. Wilhelmina and her companion were successful in raising enough money and convent furnishings to render Maria Zell more like home and to build a modest little schoolhouse with a pot-bellied stove to warm it.

In the course of this cross-continent journey, they met one of Wilhelmina's old friends in Fon-du-lac. Father Joseph Fessler had aged prematurely in the years since Wilhelmina had seen him and he was too sick, the doctor had told him, to remain in a harsh climate like Wisconsin's. His housekeeper, a very gracious and devout lady, whose cherished dream was to become a nun, cooked at the rectory to support her sister Rose and her widowed mother. This was Anna Theisen, who was destined to become Wilhelmina's superior at Beaverton for many years.

At some point near the end of her journey, Wilhelmina received a letter from Sublimity, urging her to return as soon as possible. Father Werner was critically ill, the letter said. He was in fact dying from consumption. The two Sisters hurried back, via Spokane Falls, which burned up less than a year later, arriving in Portland in late autumn, when the trees were bare and the skies as dark as slate.

The Death of Father Werner

On New Year's Day, 1889, Father Werner died. When he did not appear for Mass, they found him in his bed. "You have Father Werner," the Archbishop had said. Now he was gone and they were more alone than ever.

Father Fessler received this news in Fon-du-lac with a grim suggestion of "opportunity-is-knocking." He decided to visit Maria Zell to appraise its potential as a refuge from his semi-arctic winters in Wisconsin. He could serve as the convent chaplain, a proposal that was highly endorsed by Wilhelmina, who suggested it to the Archbishop. Gross agreed, and made a proposal of his own. Perhaps Father Fessler could arrange to bring with him Mrs. Theisen and her two daughters, Rose and Anna. The latter could realize her dream by becoming a Sister at Maria Zell. All three would fit in somewhere.

Orphanage Plans Announced

The Archbishop had anticipated opportunities like this. He was now prepared to announce plans for the formation of the new orphanage and of an orphanage auxiliary to support it.

On January 17, 1889, the *Catholic Sentinel* broke the news."A meeting of the ladies and gentlemen of the city," it reported, would be held on the following Sunday "to take into consideration the erection of an orphans' home and industrial school." To confirm the substance of this notice the Archbishop spoke "earnestly" at each of the mornings Masses in the cathedral. Priests in other parishes throughout Portland were directed to do the same, so curiosity, if nothing else, brought the ladies and gentlemen to the basement of the cathedral on Sunday, January 20. *The Sentinel,* much gratified by the results, stated that those "who filled the basement of the Church almost to the doors were therefore quite enthusiastic for the project."

His Excellency, with some of the clergy, swept into the hall "a little before three." When the ladies and gentlemen settled down, His Excellency "placed the project before them."

"There is a crying need for an orphan asylum in this Archdiocese," he began. He wore no spectacles and his face appeared to be pale and gaunt. "The [orphanage] now in charge of the Sisters of the Holy Name[s] is entirely inadequate to the wants of this great Archdiocese, and [has] no means of support except private charity and the Sisters' earnings." He proposed that they organize a "Society" in every parish in the state. Monthly contributions of the members of the society and "donations from the charitably disposed" would provide an assured income.

At this point, the Archbishop revealed a well-kept secret. "Five hundred acres of valuable agricultural land, the property of the Archbishop [will] be donated for this purpose. The property is on the O[regon] and C[alifornia] railway about ten miles from the city and is worth nearly $40,000."[15]

Doubtlessly a happy buzz followed upon this invigorating revelation. No one seems to have known that the property of the "Archbishop" had been purchased some twenty-eight years earlier, indeed the press reported it as a personal gift from William Gross. More significantly, perhaps, most of those present failed to comprehend the Archbishop's ultimate plan. "Buildings," he said, "are to be erected at once for a home for orphan children of both sexes, and in due time an industrial school and a reformatory will be placed on the same tract."

It would be difficult to demonstrate, though circumstantial evidence supports it, that at least one person, Mr. Levi Anderson, did not overlook an important element in the Archbishop's plan. Anderson, it seems, noted either then or later, the words "industrial school." His widow "in due time" offered to provide it. Thus it happened that these words became the occasion of endless discussions and many anxious moments for some of the successors of Archbishop Gross.

More Land Acquired

The tract of land to which the Archbishop referred in his announcement, did not appear, when examined more closely, to be suitable for the new orphanage. It lay north of the railroad, with its southern border running at an angle toward the southeast, not touching the railroad right-of-way on its southeast corner. Thus the Blanchet land did not have access to the county road several hundred feet beyond the railroad.

To remedy this situation, Gross purchased, on March 2, 1889, ten acres of land from Charlotte and George Hornbuckle for $500, which was one-third of the total amount Blanchet had paid for the 640 acres adjacent to it on the west. With this land directly on the railroad right-of-way, came an easement or corridor to the county road.[16] These ten acres were located where the General Motors plant is today, and it was on this site that the first orphanage was built.

The Board of Directors

St. Mary's Home Association, as the orphanage auxiliary was now called, recruited members and conducted meetings during the course of the months that followed. The Archbishop appointed six members of the first Board of Directors, who were as follows: John O'Connor, John Donnerberg, Luke Morgan, John Barrett, F. Dresser and James Foley.[17] With the approval of the Archbishop, they decided to begin construction of a building and to establish "memberships" throughout the state "for contributions of the sum of 25 cents per month each for the support of the orphans." A loan of ten thousand dollars was authorized and negotiated for the erection of "a suitable building." This orphanage, unlike most, would begin with a rich man's mortgage. If nothing else did, this alone would assure it of the watchful guidance of some cautious banker.

The Archbishop, meanwhile, cast about, seeking a religious order of men to supervise the project. Eventually, Father Henry Drees, the provincial of the Congregation of the Most Precious Blood in Cartagena, Ohio, responded to his request for help. This group ironically, perhaps, was the same from which Joseph Albrecht had separated himself and the Sisters at Jordan. Drees was interested in establishing his congregation in Oregon. Accepting a pig-in-a-poke, as it were, he traveled in early May 1889, to Portland to look over the Archbishop's proposal. Apparently satisfied, he remained long enough to preside over ground breaking ceremonies at the site on June 16, 1889.

For this auspicious event, five hundred people arrived, mostly by train, from Portland. At first, they goggled at the huge brick foundation, 50 by 109 feet, then listened to plans for the wooden three story structure that would be knocked together above it. Drees then addressed the group with appropriate remarks, ending them as follows: "In a few days, I will leave for my home in Ohio, probably never to return again." He would carry with him, he said, the kindest recollections of his six-weeks stay in Oregon.

Not much is known about him after that. Some weeks later he sent Father Alphonse Grussi from Beloit, Kansas, to Portland. Grussi, in his thirty-first year and seventh as a priest, detrained expectantly at the Union Station in Portland on a hot day of summer, August 2, 1889. Visions of a splendiferous children's home, surrounded by lawns and orchards, doubtlessly occupied his mind as a priest of the Archdiocese welcomed him and drove him to the cathedral residence beneath the branches of prolific trees and past homes of such elegance that he had never seen the like in Beloit. He was soon disillusioned, however. When he sallied out to Beaverton to visit the famous "Home," he saw only a big hole in the ground, the basement and foundations which Drees had dedicated in June. His job, he soon learned, was to complete the building, and to pay for it he was "to commence work of organizing branches of societies throughout the state."

Like most priests who are assigned to begging, Grussi cared little for it. He persevered in it for over a year, during which a contract for the structure was awarded by the Directors of the Home Society. This was not completed yet when he departed for Ohio, "taking the steamer to San Francisco" on February 11, 1891.

In the official records at the headquarters of his congregation in Ohio, the following report on Grussi's Oregon experience is filed: "[Father Grussi] collected money for the erection of St. Mary's Orphan House, Beaverton and superintended the erection . . . . We never found out how this was [done]. There is no head nor tail of it."[18]

Sometimes Archbishop Gross thought likewise. It was time, he decided hopefully, to call in his Sisters from Sublimity.

Father Fessler Takes Charge of Maria Zell

Joseph Fessler arrived in Sublimity on May 10, 1889, when the Archbishop's orphanage committee members were busy organizing St. Mary's Home Association. He was duly appointed as pastor of the parish and chaplain for Maria Zell. A few days later Anna Theisen, accompanied by her mother and her sister Rose, also arrived. Fessler provided for Rose and her mother, and Anna entered the novitiate as a postulant. Ten other girls entered the novitiate at the same time, forcing Wilhelmina to make adjustments that weakened convent discipline and threatened its very survival.

Fessler was not much help. Despite his reputation for being a very sick man, he soon displayed for everyone to see, how much energy he had, by interfering in convent business. Poor Wilhelmina, inexperienced in such matters, permitted herself to be dominated by him. In a brief time she no longer controlled the convent. In a desperate attempt to regain control, she informed the Archbishop that "the Sisters were in need of an intensive course in convent living by a trained religious," implying that Fessler should go back to running his parish.

The Archbishop agreed. His correspondence with the Precious Blood Sisters in O'Fallon, Missouri, produced the loan of Sister Mary Ludmilla Lagenbach as a novice mistress with authority to regulate the convent's discipline. Ludmilla arrived on May 7, 1890, and reported soon after on the conditions she found.

> *The superioress [Mother Wilhelmina] had been deposed and Father Fessler governed as Superior. His sister, who had left the Franciscan Order and was acting as his housekeeper, had the role of community assistant superior. Naturally there were many difficulties.*[19]

Ludmilla, called "Mother Ludmilla" at her own insistence, now regarded herself as in charge of the convent. Everyone, except Fessler, agreed.

This situation, created in part by Gross, who could have rectified it, was an embarrassing one for the Sisters of Maria Zell. They were in effect "novices" with an outsider formally in charge of their convent, and a chaplain with peculiar compulsions to interfere where he had neither experience nor authority.

While this strange scenario was still unfolding, the Archbishop dispatched instructions for Ludmilla to send three Sisters to teach in a small country school in Verboort, a crossroads up the Tualatin Valley, beyond Beaverton. Ludmilla made a fuss about this, saying that the Sisters were not ready and so on, but the Archbishop insisted that his instructions be obeyed. Two months later he dispatched another order to Ludmilla. She was to send four Sisters to Beaverton at once, to staff St. Mary's Orphan Home. Whatever her misgivings, Ludmilla complied, keeping to herself the annoyance she felt when her advice was ignored.

Chapter 2

The Early Years

ST. MARY'S HOME was about one mile beyond the suburban village of Beaverton. The railroad officials, sniffing about for additional business, agreed to provide a station stop there, which they graciously called St. Mary's. The exterior of the building was completed, but most of the interior was left unfinished.

Funds had been exhausted, yet the Archbishop insisted that the institution be opened. Accordingly the Sisters were designated to take charge, Sister M. Cecelia Boedigheimer, Superior, Sister M. Aloysius Bender, and Sister M. Seraphim Theisen, the young lady from Fond du Lac. They left the motherhouse at Sublimity on St. Patrick's Day, 1891.

Upon their arrival in Portland, they were met by a delegation of St. Mary's Home Association "a benevolent society," gushy ladies in big hats, and concerned gentlemen in bow ties, and were escorted to the home of John Donnerberg "ever after a faithful friend and benefactor." A bountiful repast, it was said, was served in honor of the Sisters, then, because the train to Beaverton did not leave Portland until morning, the Sisters were taken by buggy to the Dominican convent at St. Joseph's school.

The next morning, at the early bird hour of eight o'clock, the the Sisters detrained at St. Mary's. Their first impression was as bad as their last. What they saw was described with admirable detachment.

With the exception of some fifteen acres of land in the Beaverdam, there was no clearing on the six hundred acre tract. Within a thousand feet of the buildings, there was a second growth of pines and firs with dense shrubs of hazel bushes and vines, making a natural fence for protection; beyond this line the Sisters would not venture, for fear of being lost.[1]

They were buried in a wilderness! Prisoners in endless tracts of bushes and trees! Even Sublimity was paradise compared to this.

Upon examination, their new home did not rate much better, only two rooms, the kitchen and dining room, the first level had wooden floors, the rest, even the corridor was the bare earth. They were moving into a cave. The well had been dug during construction, some twenty-five feet from the house. This with the aid of a pump, was the only water available. In one of the large rooms on the main floor a vast heap of second-hand donations were piled, old bedsteads, bedding, chairs, dishes, cast off clothing with a musty smell, in fact everything imaginable in furniture and wearing apparel. From this pile they had to select their furnishings, "offerings from the poor to the poor." There were no lights.

A delegation from St. Mary's Home Association had accompanied the Sisters to help them get settled.

Everyone pitched in to make the best of it. Father Fessler had arranged to offer the first Mass in the home on the feast of St. Joseph, March 19, hence a chapel had to be arranged and the whole place scrubbed and cleaned as well as possible. Carpenters made a crude altar, which was decorated "with vines and moss in clean tin cans." The Association provided window washers, and its members helped with a "Bucket Brigade," to carry water for the cleansing. They were exhausted, but pleased when they climbed abroad the afternoon train to Portland, leaving the Sisters somewhat bewildered but still undaunted. One of them expressed the kind of holy joy they experienced in their abysmal poverty.

The only thing you could see was the blue sky and the great forests. The big fir trees came right up to the door. The song of the wind in the trees sang us to sleep and the branches of the trees awoke us at times as they brushed against the roof. The blue jay and the squirrel mingled their voices with ours as we prayed.

After Mass on St. Joseph Day, Father Fessler returned to Sublimity. He would come back, he announced, since it was the

Archbishop's intention to appoint him "Superintendent" of the Home. True to his word he arrived a few days later, bag and baggage, accompanied by "Grandma" Theisen and his sister, who had agreed to take over the sewing room of the new establishment. One can imagine that there was great rejoicing in Maria Zell that night. The absence of Fessler and his sister removed the burden of too much interference from Mother Ludmilla's long suffering.

But Sublimity's loss was Beaverton's gain. Fessler was wholly in charge now, and he soon indicated that not only was he going to run the show at St. Mary's, but he would direct it at Verboort as well. No one can doubt that he was sincere. Sincerity, alas, was not enough for harmonious relations with the Sisters during the weeks that followed.

The Sisters and The Children

Within a month of opening day, there were sixty children at the Home, both boys and girls. More help to staff the place was sent from Sublimity, creating crises in both places because of the disruption in the formation of the younger Sisters. At this time the entire congregation consisted of only twenty-two members, now living in three convents. Mother Ludmilla was alarmed. She expressed her concern to the Archbishop then waited for his proposals to resolve the dilemma.

Meanwhile, the neighbors in the valley, hearing of the arrival of the Sisters and the orphans, brought a share of what they had, vegetables, potatoes, fruit and meat. Among the most generous were Mr. & Mrs. Patrick Hyland, who initially helped by bringing food, then eventually brought their greatest treasure, their daughter Mary. As Sister Mary Xavier, one of St. Mary's overworked cooks, she labored in the kitchen in the Home for a quarter of a century, always smiling and always prayerful.

The sixty children at the Home could consume more food than members of St. Mary's Home Association realized. Their contribution of twenty-five cents a month was about all that the Superior, Sister Cecelia had to work with. Her account for the first calendar year, neatly kept in a proper book, indicated how dependent upon their neighbors and their own resources the Sisters really were.

**March 19, 1891 to January 1, 1892
Sisters of Precious Blood in Acct.**

Potatoes	$15.80
Carrots and beets	$ 7.00
Apples	$ 6.00
Sauerkraut and barrels	$ 7.50
Turnips and cabbage	$ 9.00
Dried apples	$ 5.40
Vinegar	$ 4.75
Pork	$ 7.75
Groceries	$15.20
Wool	$11.75
Repairing shoes	$ 7.85
Potatoes	$14.00
Med. for children and cattle	$ 4.75
Poultry	$ 9.00
Cabbage	$ 7.00
Barrels	$ 6.00
Rep[air] shoes	$ 5.50
Clothing	$ 5.75
Freight	$32.40
TOTAL:	$182.40[2]

"It is well that the Sisters were young and strong," wrote the convent historian, "for there was much work to do — sixty growing children to feed, to clothe, and to keep clean, and no conveniences." The laundry had to be done by hand. On Mondays, wash day, the Sisters rose at 3:30 in the morning, said their prayers and made their meditation. At 4:30 they were ready to do the washing. Each Sister had a tub and a wash stand. Making bread was another ordeal.

"Every morning while I [Sister Cecelia] had charge of the kitchen, I arose at 4:30. The boys and girls helped me before school. A boy and I worked the bread each day. We baked twenty-five to thirty loaves daily. In the afternoon I baked biscuits and other things."[3]

"The orchards were just planted so they had no fruit of their own. During the summer, the Sisters took all of the older children out to the woods to gather blackberries, huckleberries, blue berries and wild strawberries. In the autumn they gathered sacks of hazel nuts. "The berries were needed to flavor the dry bread in the winter time and the nuts came back at Christmas time in little red sacks."

"We were very poor and it was many years before the Sisters or the children tasted butter, sugar or eggs. Later these were Sunday delicacies. Some of the Sisters used to save their Christmas candy to put into the applesauce that it might not be so sour for the children and the Sisters. Farmers from Verboort and Cedar Mills brought us many loads of fruit and vegetables."

"Of the nearly square mile of land surrounding the Home, only fifteen acres "of rich beaver dam" were cleared for garden use. "All the [cleared] land that was not needed for garden was planted in onions. Here the bigger children would work after school, making the woods echo with their gay laughter."

"How hard we worked in that onion patch and how hot the sun baked our backs!" Here all the early Sisters of St. Mary spent days practicing the motto of the young Community "orare et laborare." But the onions grew big and the prices were high in those days. The sale of the onions was a great help in supporting the orphans.

But the money, whatever its source, was never enough. Two Sisters had to go out to beg, traveling throughout the state to glean what they could.

Often they were most kindly received but sometimes also they were treated with contempt and scorn. The roads were muddy, conveyances poor; thus their trips were often tedious and uncomfortable. Several times they seemed in danger of death; but it was all done gladly for God's little ones.[4]

During the second year, Father Fessler reported, the Sisters spent a total of $1,033.10. It should be noted, perhaps, that this represented a cash outlay of something like $17.21 for each child for a whole year. At this rate, the three dollar annual contributions of only 344 families in all of Oregon could have kept the Home solvent and the beggar Sisters in the convent.

Although Fessler was severe with the children and too bossy with the Sisters, he was entirely dedicated to his work. He lived as poorly as the rest and he was faithful in performing his spiritual duties for the Sisters. As superintendent he attended to the development of the land and care of the building. Under his supervision the older boys slashed the brushwood on both sides "of the beaver dam," opening a much larger area for gardening. To obtain a supply of better water, he contracted for a new well, deep and lined with brick, and above it a two-story tower containing an adequate reservoir. Above the tower a windmill whirred in the breeze, pumping a great supply of water which was piped into the building. "Great was the joy over the improvement."

Then there was the unsolved problem of the floors. About this time a professional carpenter appeared, a William Holzhausen by name. He offered his services for board and room and five dollars a month. Fessler gladly accepted him and put him to work on the floors "in all of the rooms, so that the Sisters no longer had to stand on the wet ground to do the family washing." In these and many other ways, Fessler proved to be a valued help to the Sisters and the orphans, but Mother Ludmilla, who had a stubborn streak of her own, found it difficult to accept him.

Ludmilla was living now at the Home. In consultation with the Archbishop, she decided at last to move the Maria Zell novitiate to St. Mary's, where the younger Sisters could help in the management of the Home. On the Feast of Our Lady of Perpetual Help, a special occasion for Redemptorists, [June 27, 1891], the move was accomplished with impeccable order and German efficiency. The professed Sisters, except those left behind to teach in Sublimity, the novices and the postulants, sixteen in all, moved into the orphanage "temporarily" into a large unused classroom, which became a combination community room and office for Sister Superior. They remained there for about three years, that is until the new motherhouse was built a quarter of a mile away.

First Profession At St. Mary's

Ludmilla stoically faced what she regarded as an intolerable task. There were twelve in the novitiate to be given the elementary training for living a religious life, there were the professed Sisters, some of them still quite immature and in need of direction, then there were the children who required complete personal care, as well as an elementary school education. There were two parochial schools, to be staffed and supervised. All this was to be done with a very limited personnel of trained Sisters.

At first Ludmilla made the best of it. On the surface it was business as usual. The Archbishop, who regarded his orphanage as the apple of his eye, came out from Portland occasionally and spent the evening with the Sisters. "The Community would assemble and His Excellency, in his kind paternal way, would give a conference on the religious life and virtues, or relate some of the experiences of his missionary life." Three postulants, who had been transferred from Sublimity to St. Mary's, were presented by Ludmilla to the Archbishop for entrance into the novitiate. He appointed the day, July 6, 1891, Feast of the Most Precious Blood, for the ceremony, the first at St. Mary's. Father Fessler celebrated high Mass *Coram Episcopo* after which His Excellency presided over the reception, according to the ritual of the Precious Blood Sisters at O'Fallon. The names of the three postulants are significant: Rose Theisen, Sister Seraphim's younger sister, who entered the convent when she was only thirteen years old; Frances Heuberger from Sublimity; and, Catherine Sweeney "from Ireland." The religious names they chose were Sister Mary Engratia, Sister Mary Theresa and Sister Mary Frances.

The ceremony was an inspiration for everyone, but it did not alter the basic conflict within the community, which was, of course, Fessler's gratuitous usurpation of the functions and authority of the religious superior. Ludmilla did her best to portion out the duties to the Sisters, with due regard to the abilities and strength of each; her freedom, however, was greatly hampered by the superintendent, who now had closer contact with the Sisters than before. "He dictated where they were to be placed and what their tasks in that place were to be. He showed small regard for the fact that (Ludmilla) was superior by ecclesiastical appointment and much better equipped to do the task well. Mother Ludmilla submitted quietly for the sake of peace with never a word of complaint to the Sisters, though they often saw her leaving his office with tears in her eyes."

"The priest acted as superior in all three places," she revealed later, referring explicitly to Sublimity as well as Verboort and Beaverton. There was no point in these circumstances for her to remain in Oregon. Suddenly on June 27, 1892, Mother Ludmilla, wishing the Sisters at St. Mary God's blessing and a fond farewell, departed for Portland en route to Missouri. Once again these hapless Sisters felt betrayed, not by Mother Ludmilla, but by the very ones who loved them most and in whom they had placed all their trust.

Life At The Home
According to Lawrence Farnsworth

Among the first children, the third on the register, was a precocious little fellow, who became the domestic pet, along with the dog Pedro. Lawrence Farnsworth was only two months old when he arrived on March 18, 1891, one day after the Sisters' arrival. He remained thirteen years, and many more years later, when he was a distinguished reported for the *New York Times,* he composed a lengthy account about his Boys' Home memories.[5]

First he described the Home as he remembered it:

> *My first impression of "the Home" was that it was painted a pale fading blue. It faced a wide open space which at various times was partly a lawn with flowers and partly a vegetable garden. Just beyond this space was the railroad track where there was a train each way from and to Portland in the morning and again in the evening.*
>
> *If you stood in this space and looked at the building you saw a very wide wooden stairway leading up to the main entrance squarely in the building's center. It opened on a porch with white balustrades which ran around the front and two sides of the second story. A porch just like it ran around the story above it. The fourth story was above that. In the center of the fourth*

St. Mary's Home with motherhouse in background.

story facade there was also a niche for a statue, but at that time no statue. The building had a slightly slanting tin roof. From a flat space at the top of the roof there was a kind of rounded pavilion topped by a cupola. You could climb onto this flat space by a ladder from the attic and then climb into the pavilion and look around . . . .

When I was about six or seven years old a crew of painters came and started scraping off the blue paint, after which they repainted the building a kind of slate grey, and the niche bright blue. After that a white statue of the Blessed Virgin Mary was raised into the niche, and below it an inscription, "Hail Mary, full of grace," and perhaps a few more words after that.

There were three stairways on the interior. The main stairway was squarely in the center and went up from the basement with a landing on each floor. It has polished banisters down which the boys liked to slide, although they were forbidden to do so. There was an open space between the banisters and the floors so you could look straight down to the basement from the top floor. One day a boy named Archie Murphy was sliding down the top banister when he lost his balance and dropped straight down to the basement. He was badly hurt but I don't believe any bones or parts of the skull were broken and he got over it. He was nicknamed "Spud" Murphy. Some of the boys said he ate so many potatoes that the potatoes came out of him when he hit the floor, which at that time was wooden.

On the second floor, starting from the east and along the front side of the house were the priest's room which also served as the business office; then the priest's bedroom, the parlor for visitors, the lobby off the main entrance, the chapel. The boys knelt or sat on one side of the chapel, the Sisters on the other. At first there were only kneeling benches for the small boys, and some chairs back of that. When the small boys weren't kneeling they sat on the benches. There were chairs on the other side for the Sisters because it was plain they couldn't very well sit on kneeling benches like the small boys. Later on, about 1900 or even earlier, pews were installed on both sides — which seem a most modern touch, if not an extravagance. In the rear, on the Sisters' side, which was the side next to the windows, was a raised square platform in the center of which was the pedal organ around which the Sisters' choir gathered during mass and benediction. It was too bad that the Sisters' side was next to the windows, because it kept the boys from looking out of the window and observing the beauties of nature and the passing trains while they prayed.

Two great oil lamps were hung from the ceiling. Most of the rooms in the building had ornate round plaster disks which were part of the ceilings, and in the center of each disk was a hook for the hanging of a lamp.

The Kitchen and Refectory

Along one side of the corridor on the basement floor, starting from the west end, was the kitchen with a long range, heated by a wood fire. It was quite a job keeping the big wood box filled. The boys, myself included, took turns carrying in armsful of wood. At one end of the range was a big kneading bowl for bread making, and behind that a sink for the washing of dishes. Sister Mary Magdalen did most of the kneading and baking. Sister Agatha was a frequent assistant. There were several large tables in the kitchen, and beyond that a narrow pantry which opened on the Sisters' refectory. Outside that was a hallway for the main stairway, and a room at the back which was used now and then as a bathroom. The building had no bathtubs then as it had later when more adequate plumbing was installed. So the boys had to bathe once in a while in big round wooden washtubs borrowed from the laundry.

I suppose the next most important place of rendezvous was the refectory in the basement opposite the kitchen. Long tables stretched along each side of the room. There were benches on each side of the tables and there the boys sat. The table was set with tin plates and cups. We ate mostly with spoons — what there was in the way of knives and forks I don't remember. The fare was plain — very plain. Almost always potatoes, sometimes fried in a very large square pan from which they were served, or boiled with or without jackets, or mashed with a generous assortment of lumps. Hash was frequent and sometimes there was stew and gravy which was spread over the bread. It was good homemade bread, none of the anemic bleached flour stuff that comes from bakeries today. There was one slice of bread for each boy. For dessert there was most frequently applesauce, or stewed dried prunes or apples, and in the season fresh fruit. Milk, eggs or butter were unknown commodities. These, like sugar, were luxuries. There was always coffee, made out of roasted barley or oats. It was brown, showing that milk had been put into it before serving. Yes the food was indeed plain but it was nourishing and the boys thrived. They always seemed to have boundless energy and health.

The Barnyard

Farther away to the left you also caught glimpses of other beaver dam lands that belonged to "The Home," of two bridges that spanned them; of forests and woodland partly cleared, of fields, of a complex of farm buildings. One of these was called the wagon shed because the lower part was wide open and there wagons and farm machinery was stationed when not in use. But it had an enclosed upper story, more like an attic, which was put to various uses — for storing things I believe.

What was fascinating about this building in the springtime was the arrival of the mud swallows, hundreds of them. They built their mud nests under the eves, so close together that there seemed hardly a knife's breadth between them. Through the spring and the summer they flew busily in and out; darted at each other in play, chased invisible insects. In the late fall they flew away. The mud nests remained behind during the winter, gradually vanishing, so that in the following spring the nest building had to be started all over again.

The main woodshed was quite a gathering place for the boys on rainy days and often on Sundays. Sometimes the workmen complained of the noise they made on Sundays because that, said the men, was their day for sleeping and rest. Behind "The Home" and the woodshed was another drab building, an outhouse called "the toilet" used by everybody before the installation of the appropriate plumbing.

Back of the barn was a corral where the cows and sheep stood about after being driven in from the pastures, and before returning thereto in the morning. In this yard there was also a well with a pump, and a drinking trough. It was at somewhat later time, under Father Heinrich, that a pig pen was built, a long building with low slanting roofs, with well-constructed and relatively clean compartments, and a huge iron cooking vat under which a fire was built. This was next to the chicken house.

The smallest of all buildings was Pedro's doghouse, near the sidewalk that led to the convent. Pedro was a black collie, on the aging side, gentle and a favorite of the children. He was fed scraps of meat and other food in a big dish by the doghouse. There was no such thing as buying prepared dog food — that

Operation of the farm was important to the Home's survival.

would have been an unheard-of extravagance. One day Pedro disappeared. This caused much concern. Droves of boys roamed the woods in various directions ringing a bell and calling "Here Pedro! Here Pedro!" Pedro never responded.

The open space was mostly grass-covered but farther away were garden patches, especially a cabbage patch. There was usually some kind of activity. Closer in toward town was the area reserved for the girls' playground. They amused themselves in various ways, walking, running, talking, playing some games like tag or ring games and their own invention of baseball much scorned by the boys.

The Old Orchard sloped down to grassy bottom land beyond which was the shallow lily pond, the only pond in the whole property, and to one side the swimming hole, a widened and deeper part of the creek which was assuming the proportions of a small river.

In the lily pond grew reeds and cattails and large petaled bright yellow water lilies with green knobby centers and black-purple fringe surrounding the knobs at their base. They grew on thick, rubbery stems. They had no resemblances to the white flowers on ponds in other parts of the country which also are *called water lilies. The pond was something used for wading — it was probably not more than thigh deep at its deepest. But there were so many attractive wading places in the creeks 'round about, that the pond was not very enticing.*

The Archbishop and His Orphans

These lively remarks by Farnsworth reveal a different scenario of Catholic orphanages than the nineteenth century stereotype. Oliver Twist would have been very happy at St. Mary's and there is reason to believe that most of the children were.

Farnsworth's comments about the Home's top V.I.P.'s leave little doubt about his own favored status. He presented both in the best possible light. "I remember Archbishop Gross," he wrote, "as a spare, dark, warm-hearted and folksy sort." Several times he sat on the Archbishop's lap. "I was one of his favorites," he added. The Archbishop came by train from Portland, and when it was known that he was on the way, the boys and girls dressed in their best clothes and lined up in two rows, facing each other along the walk that led up from the track to the gate. They were lined up also on the front stairs to the porch. Gross went up the stairs, barely recognizing their presence, through the main entrance and through the hall into the chapel. "There he knelt before seeing anyone."

Sometimes the Archbishop attended the entertainments which the children provided in one of the classrooms. "He seemed to enjoy these very amateurish affairs, after [which] he would give a nice talk."

Not all of the programs were successful. One of these was intended to be very special for the friends and benefactors of the Home, to show them what "The Home" was like and "what its children were doing." Many hand-written invitations were sent out. On the appointed day, a Sunday, all watched the morning train from Portland, "and sure enough when it came there was a great outpouring of passengers. But alas, they were not guests to whom invitations had gone. They were all Italians who had come for the baptism of the baby of an Italian truck gardener living at Beaverton." For the entertainment, which had been produced with weeks of elaborate preparations "there may have been one guest." None others responded. "The entertainment was given, of course . . . but an aura of disappointment prevailed."

Father Fessler

Farnsworth's ready acceptance of Father Fessler appears to be in sharp contrast with that of Mother Ludmilla. "I must have been only three or four years old when I became perceptively aware of Father Joseph Fessler. He was German, somewhat corpulent, jovial and kindly . . . but [he] impressed me as having considerable capacity for taking hold of things and making them go. Certainly he made the farm a going affair."

The priest's room, he said, was his office and living room. "Here he sat at a long desk in the corner, the desk topped with dark green pebbled leather, with a window on the left side and a front window just at the edge of the desk on the right. Both windows looked on the porch. In the opposite corner was another desk, surmounted by a tall, light-yellow book cabinet with glass doors, the cabinet reaching within two feet of the ceiling. The floor was carpeted wall to wall, straw under the carpet."

One can picture Fessler's room, the best in the house. Most of its contents had been moved from Wisconsin to Oregon; the desks, the cabinets with the glass doors, the carpet. The straw would keep the floor warm, if the carpet did not. Breathing heavily at his cherished desk, topped with its green leather, Fessler could conduct his little empire. If not a saint, he was at least a good priest, who lived righteously according to his own dated understanding of justice and charity.

Farnsworth remembered his books and how they did not matter any more, after their owner had died.

> *Here Father Fessler transacted business and received callers. On his desk were various kinds of paper, in rather orderly fashion. He always spoke in German with whomsoever he treated. I was privileged to come in there and, by the hour, play on the floor under the tables. He seemed pleased to have me around. I had my ears open, heard all that was said and tried to read meaning into what I heard.*
>
> *Father Fessler must have been something of a scholar. In one of the rooms on another part of this floor, many books, which seemed very old, were on the shelves lining the wall. I remember these being sorted out and packed after his death.*

As you have doubtlessly guessed, this boy Farnsworth had a big mouth, as well as a good memory. His reports on other subjects confirm both judgements and add some choice reflections on the behavior of sharp-eyed children of every age and place.

His Observations on Sundry Subjects

At the Christmas dinner there was special food like turkey, duck, goose or chicken . . . donated by farmers' round about. [These were] served mainly stewed or roasted. Some [children] got one kind, some another, according to what was on hand. There was cake and special desserts . . . but there was never such luxury as ice cream. I never tasted it as long as I was at the Home.

Christmas Toys

Among other toys was a toy piano. One of the children names Vincent Connelly was fascinated by it. He would sit on a stool and play it for hours and sing his own kind of songs — songs invented by him with few if any regular dictionary words. The older people who came into the room were struck by his singing, talked about it and said he would probably grow up into a celebrated singer. I didn't see how his singing was any better than mine. Sometimes I pointed out that I could sing too, and give demonstrations. No one ever applauded.

Santa Claus

The next day there was much discussion about Santa Claus and a few of the boys said there wasn't any. This was hotly disputed by other boys who had seen him in person, they said. "Well," some of the heretical group said, "seems to us that Santa Claus has a voice like Sister Laurentia." I was half convinced when I heard that — but only half.

The Ragman

At this time a ragman used to come out from Portland in a junky wagon drawn by a tired and dispirited horse to buy rags. There was always a collection of rags in gunny sacks waiting for him and he hooked a pair of scales on each sack and weighed it. One day I went along beside his wagon to open the gates. At the last gate he told me what a fine boy I was and said I deserved a reward. He reached into a pocket and brought out a small dirty purse. I had visions of at least a quarter. Ostentatiously he handed me a penny. When he was out of sight I buried the penny in the ground and there perhaps it still lies.

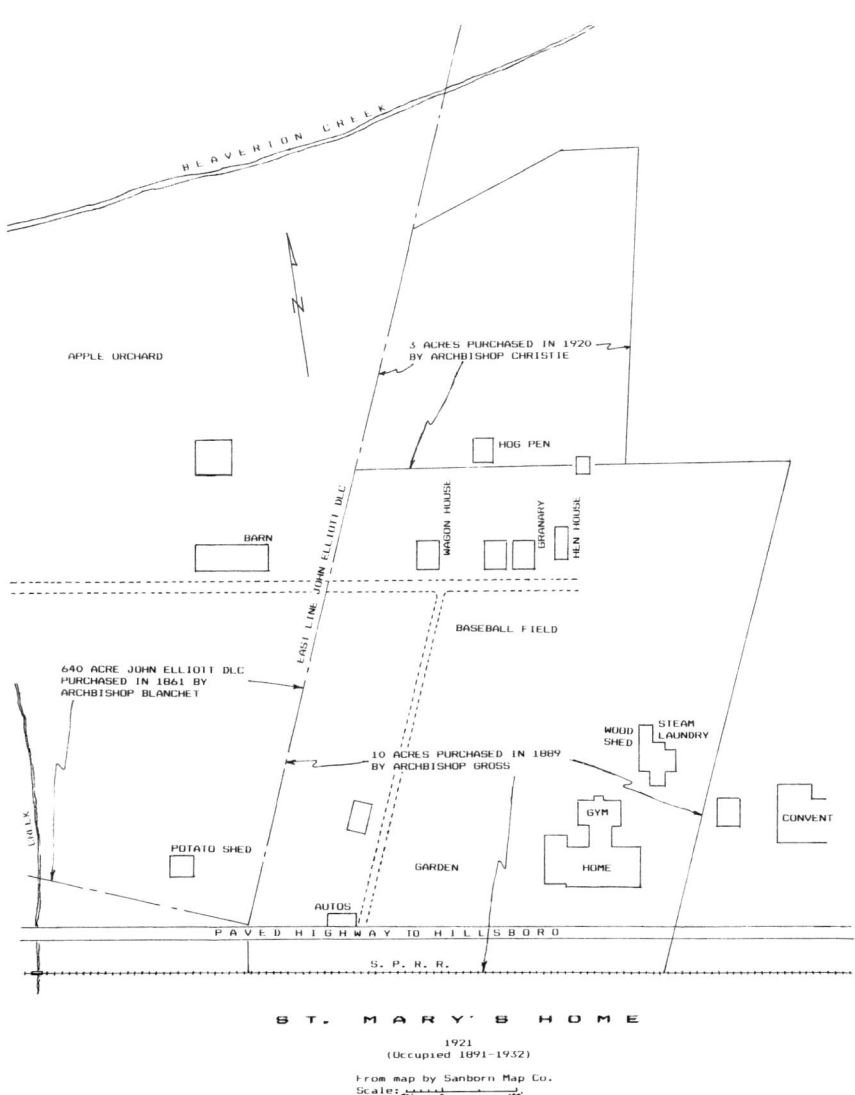

St. Mary's Home for Boys — 1921

A small boy has his dignity, after all. The next time the ragman came I remembered to put a brick in two of the rag bags before they got weighed.

The Shoes Day

About once a year there was a distribution of shoes in the refectory. The shoes came in a huge wooden crate, all in a jumble. I believe they were odd lots and remnants sent by one of the Portland department stores. The shoes were spread out on the floor and the boys picked and chose and tried on one pair or another for size. When a boy found the right size, that pair was his. Once I must have picked out a pair more for fancy appearance than size. For quite some time thereafter they were painful. But in time shoes and feet became used to each other.

The Trains

Also in the mornings you could see the train outbound from Portland, circling the low hills; you traced its movements by the white smoke. The train passed St. Mary's about 8:30. It went as far as Corvallis, nearly 100 miles, which seemed a great distance, and came back in the evening. There was also an evening train from Portland which went as far as Sheridan which was on a branch line from the main line and not so distant. That train came back in the morning. There was an hour's difference between the passing of the up and down trains, both mornings and evenings. St. Mary's was a flag stop.

While on this subject another incident comes to mind. The train that passed by Portland bound — or the reverse — had cars lighted with oil lamps and heated by a round, upright coal stove at one end in a corner. Cars were right cozy that way. Once I was taken on the train with one of the Sisters Portland bound. It was a dark wintry evening and we had a seat somewhere in the middle of the car. Then the conductor, a man with a dark shriveled face, a black mustache and a kindly manner, came along and said, "Bring the little girl up by the fire." I was indignant and shouted, "I'm not a little girl — I'm a boy!" Everybody in the car laughed — and I seethed with fury.

The New Superior General

On June 29, 1892, the feast of St. Peter and Paul, Sister M. Seraphim was elected as Superior General of the Sisters' Congregation.

Only twenty-three years old and one of the three Sisters on the Home's staff, she had received the stamp of approval from Father Fessler, who still favored his doughty cook from Fon-du-lac. Perhaps Fessler had interfered by sharing his thoughts on the subject. If so, it was a small matter compared to some of his decisions.

Seraphim was no whimp. Her small, thin mouth set firmly in an oval shaped face, and her dark eyes, like a Spanish mystic, suggested that she was born to rule. In those eyes there was evidence of great inner strength. No one, not even Father Fessler, would tell her how to run the congregation. He no doubt realized this since he had known her longer than any of the Sisters. Whatever the effect of his influence on her election, she began briskly to make needed changes at the orphanage.

Of greatest importance was a new convent for the Sisters, a separate motherhouse, which the Sisters could claim as their own on land of their own. This obviously required the acquisition of land and Seraphim, like Fessler, cast eyes on the neighbor's farm east of the original tract bought by Archbishop Blanchet. This neighbor, of course was Hornbuckle. According to Farnsworth, who was sometimes too big for his britches, the Sisters were trying to convert him. Farnsworth had this to say about him.

> *In a far corner of the woodland opposite the convent lived "Old Man Hornbuckle," as the boys called him. His low sprawling house was hidden from view from the convent. An access road ran through his property to the county road and you had to open a gate to get onto that highway. George Hornbuckle had a rather short white beard and white sideburns, in fact a white hairy face. He was kindly enough in his way but complained about the carelessness of the boys on his property, especially when they left the gate open or perhaps got into his fruit trees. He had wooded land but not much in the way of a farm. He lived mostly alone. I used to see a teen-age girl come and go from his place. I am sure she wasn't his daughter, but she probably looked after him, because at his age he needed someone around.*
>
> *Mr. Hornbuckle had an adopted son named Billy who, in my time, did not live with him but in Portland. Sometimes he came out on a visit. He was quite a "dude," dressed as though he had stepped out of a bandbox. I admired his sharply pressed navy*

blue trousers. His speech seemed somewhat affected, like the speech of some actors. Sometimes on his visits I flagged the train for him but I don't think he ever gave me a nickel. One day he showed me and one or two other boys in the gravel platform what he described as a right modern and handy invention — a fountain pen. I had never seen or even heard of anything like that.

Mr. Hornbuckle had friendly relations with the Sisters. Sometimes a couple of Sisters would visit him to see if he was all right and bring him delicacies. The Sisters sense of public relations was good — they knew how to get along with the mostly Protestant people of Beaverton and surrounding communities.

Then came the word that Mr. Hornbuckle was very ill and almost certain to die very soon. Sisters visited him every day. They had set their hearts on converting him and having him baptized before death. But he had his own established convictions. He declined to be converted. "I want to die as I have lived," he told the Sisters.

Hornbuckle did not die then, and not for some time. He lived long enough to try to take advantage of the Sisters, but he under estimated their sagacious sense of business and lost all he had hoped to profit from them.

Eventually the Sisters bought seven and one-half acres from him and in June 1893 they started construction on their new motherhouse. This was completed in January of the following year. Archbishop Gross came to dedicate the place on January 18, which was a Thursday in that year. The sun, despite predictions to the contrary, appeared brightly in a blue sky and warmed the air agreeably. The children at the Home, granted an unforeseen holiday, were beside themselves with joy, but they paid dearly for it. An ordeal of three hours at the dedication services tended to curb their high spirits. There was compensation, however, in an elaborate "eye-opening" dinner, which the boys grossly called "a feed."

One of the best features of the dedication was the departure from the Home of all the Sisters, except those on the orphanage staff. This left more room for the children and fewer adults to supervise them, which was interpreted favorably, even with mischievous delight by some.

The New Motherhouse

For Seraphim and her Sisters, the new motherhouse was a triumph. They were very proud of it and they gussied it up with flowers, trees and other attractions, including, in the course of time, a chicken yard. Farnsworth was pleased with it all and he wrote later about it with confidence though he was only in his fourth year when it was occupied.

> Up to this point I have only passingly referred to the convent, called the motherhouse. The motherhouse was eastward on ground that belonged to the Sisters. It was reached from "The Home" by a narrow sidewalk, perhaps 400 yards long. On each side of the walk were gardens. At one time a prune orchard was planted in the field next to the railroad track, which belonged to "The Home." On each side of the walk were rows of flowers — geraniums, "Sweet Williams," small carnations called "pinks," sweet peas and so on. The Sisters took pleasure in making things look pretty.
>
> In the convent's back yard there were two, perhaps three buildings close in, reached by a sidewalk. One was the chicken house and yard, the yard having the usual high fence to keep in the chickens. Next to the far outside corner of the yard were several beehives. When the bees swarmed and flew off in the summer they were followed with a ringing of bells, a beating of cans and much shouting by the boys until they settled down somewhere on the limb of a tree or elsewhere. The theory was that if you made enough noise the bees wouldn't fly very far. After they settled they were scooped into another hive. Thus the population explosion went on year after year.

Father Fessler's Last Years

The convent's control over the bees was symbolic of Fessler's control over the Home; it was slipping away. Age had little to do with this, Fessler was only in his fifty-first year at this time. But sickness and grinding poverty of the Home had worn him down. Time has a way of resolving most problems, but it often makes poverty worse. The Home Association, for all its good intentions, brought in less and less cash as the months progressed, while the number of the children and costs of operations climbed up with the inevitability of cloudy skies. The Archbishop could see the red ink on the records as well as Fessler, and he was persuaded, at last, to assign one of his priests as an official beggar for the Home.

Father John Schell was the lucky man. He could beg all day and all week and could use his official splendiferous title: State Traveling Agent. One wonders how he merited so much prestige.

A popular magazine called *McClures* had been engaged for some time in exposing scandals in the logging industry in Oregon. The great "Lumber Barons," it was alleged, were guilty of vast land frauds throughout the state. In *McClure* articles on this subject Father John Schell's name surfaced with striking regularity. Recognized as a member of the Catholic clergy, he was deeply resented by some powerful members of the lumber industry, who, one suspects, had the last word on the nature of his future activities. It was openly stated that "he had made enemies."

Schell, it was said, had "a rugged physique and seemed outwardly gruff." He was as tough as he appeared to be. Later, Archbishop Christie assigned him and several other priests to parishes in eastern Oregon, then cut them loose from Portland by promoting the establishment of the Diocese of Baker City (1903). Schell was conspicuous in his belligerent opposition.[6] Another priest, like Schell in his opposition, was Father Joseph Heinrich, who succeeded Fessler as Superintendent of the Home.

As far as the kids in the Home were concerned, Schell was a hero. He had a soft spot in his heart for them. He visited the Home when he was able, "bringing big wooden buckets of candy each time." His popularity with the kids revealed his true personality which helped to make him a success as a beggar. It was generally believed that he was "very successful," and the *Catholic Sentinel* in December 1894, happily reported a triumph at Gervais. Schell grossed $62.40, a handsome pot for those days.

If this sounds like peanuts, it really was. The cost for operating the Home that year was less than $500.00 in cash, in addition to the produce of the farm and other gifts in kind, like the labor of the Sisters who were unsalaried. Fessler had some undeclared money stashed away, but like some other Germans I know, he was saving it for a rainy day, overlooking the heavy showers in his front yard.

His health, never robust, began to decline noticeably. He suffered from dropsy, it was said, a medical disorder now called edema.

Knowledgeable people call it "a symptom of disease rather than the disease itself." In effect it caused an abnormal accumulation of bodily fluid so that Fessler appeared to be somewhat bloated looking. He tried earnestly to diet, with little success, in part for the lack of sufficient protein. As his decline began to impair his activities, he summoned his brother Charles, a priest in Wisconsin, to assist him.

Charles arrived in early January 1896. Then for five lingering months he watched his brother die. The end came quietly on June 21, 1896.

The solemn funeral, a major sensation for the kids, was conducted by Archbishop Gross in the chapel in the Home. "The Chapel altar and the wall behind it," Farnsworth wrote later, "were draped in black." What with the black habits of the many Sisters, the black vestments of the Bishop and his priests and the black draperies, not to mention the black coffin, the place looked like a scene from "Faust." This was not high on the kids' choices for entertainment.

When the Archbishop spoke he said that Father Fessler "was not only a good priest, but he was also a humble and submissive priest. He had no pride of opinion, nor arrogance of ambition. He was to obey wherever duty lay; and therefore, standing here before the Altar of God, I pronounce him a faithful priest, and a most worthy man." All of the children and the Sisters marched to the grave in procession "and witnessed the consignment of the body to the earth." Little Farnsworth was "deeply impressed" and felt the sorrow of it, but he did not think that he wept.

Seraphim Buys More Land

During recreation in the motherhouse in the years that followed, the Sisters knitted or crocheted while they offered pious comments about their "sainted" Father Fessler. Some Sisters thought that they now had two patrons in heaven, Werner and Fessler, but others were a bit skeptical about the latter. They thought that Fessler had been derelict in holding the money they had begged without their knowledge. He had turned it over before his death and this, with the estate he willed to the Sisters, totalled something like six thousand dollars.

For Seraphim the details posed no problem. She needed money and this windfall looked like a million dollars. Her first priority in its use was the acquisition of more land for the convent, a very wise decision as time would tell. Since Mr. Hornbuckle had sold the Sisters seven and one-half acres earlier, she sought him now with a proposal that he sell them another sixty acres.

In 1903 he finally consented to Seraphim's request, thinking as he gleefully informed some of his cronies, that the Sisters would never be able to pay for it. He would get it back eventually, he said, so that he could sell it again. In this the Old Man misjudged his neighbors, just as they had misjudged his willingness to be converted. When he delivered title upon completion of payment, the Sisters owned sixty acres of good land, on the opposite side of the railroad track from their convent, along the county road from Beaverton to Hillsboro. This important, but muddy artery was flanked with enormous billboards, advertising "Pearline" and "Horseshoe" chewing tobacco, snuff and "Owl" cigars, "Wizard Oil," and other products of interest.

Chapter 3

The Years of Peaceful Survival

During the last months of the superintendent's illness, Mother Seraphim directed the daily operations of the Home. Fessler's brother Charles filled in as chaplain, as occasion required, and agreed to remain until the Archbishop found another priest who was available and willing to head up the impecunious and over crowded institution. Recognizing this as a suitable interim arrangement, His Excellency formalized it with the following document.

> *St. Mary's Home: June 23, 1896.*
> *To All Whom It May Concern: Whereas during the last four months of the life of our dear deceased Rev. Jos.Fessler, the Mother Superioress, Sister Seraphina [sic] — was entrusted with the account books, and management of the interior affairs of the St. Mary's Home, we hereby wish and order that she continue in the same office and duties until the arrangements proper to be made definitely to supply the vacancy caused by the death of our dear Rev. Jos. Fessler — are duly constituted — For outside business during this same interval, we constitute Rev. Chas. Fessler — as business manager —*
> *In witness whereof*
>
> +Wm. H. Gross
Archbip. Oregon[1]

He finally selected for the director's position Father John Heinrich, the gloomy Austrian-born priest, who appears to have been burnt out with parish work before he arrived at the Home.

Heinrich had been ordained by Archbishop Blanchet in Portland's pro-Cathedral soon after the first Vatican Council. He had distinguished himself as a missionary pastor in the Roseburg area of southwestern Oregon, then as "rector" of St. Francis Church in Baker City, and finally for four years as "rector" of St. Francis Church in east Portland. While at the latter, he faithfully attended the famous middle-weight prize fighter, Jack Dempsey during his last sickness. On November 7, 1895, the *Catholic Sentinel* reported this first Jack Dempsey's death: "[He] died at the home of his wife's parents, Mr. and Mrs. James Brady, 393 Grand Avenue, Friday morning, after illness from consumption, aged 33 . . . . The funeral took place from St. Francis church, and was perhaps the largest that had been witnessed in Portland for some time." Heinrich was the celebrant of the funeral Mass which attracted "many hundreds" and caused a traffic jam of horse drawn carriages.

For a brief time, Heinrich was almost a celebrity, a role, which did little to lessen his troubles with his own health. It is very probable that Gross assigned him to be the new superintendent and chaplain for the Sisters on the naive assumption that his health would improve in the country air. He arrived at St. Mary's Home on October 1, 1896, and moved somewhat reluctantly, it may be presumed, into Fessler's former quarters.

Archbishop Alexander Christie

The third Archbishop of Oregon City, William Gross, had died in Baltimore on the early morning of November 14, 1898. He had been feeling unwell for some time. He was not an old man, only sixty one, but he was a tired one. He had been a Bishop for twenty-five years, which was like running a railroad for fifty.

On August 15, 1898, he presided at the motherhouse for the vow ceremony of two Sisters. Several weeks later he returned again to Beaverton to present to the Sisters "a large case of Altar linen." With premonitions of his death, perhaps, he revealed for the first time "that he had suffered much for them" because of the opposition of most of his priests to the new congregation, the Sisters of St. Mary. He added that he had prayed much and firmly believed "that the right course had been chosen . . . then he blessed them and went his way."

Gross had not told all. Like Father Fessler, he was suffering acutely from a heart condition, from which he died, unexpectedly, only four months later.

There was much speculation in rectories about his successor. The suspense ended with the announcement that Bishop Alexander Christie of Vancouver Island had been elevated to Oregon City as its fourth Archbishop. Christie did not occupy his see until June 23, 1899. In the four months interim, Oregon Catholics, especially the clergy, assiduously sought clues regarding his likes and dislikes, and especially his peculiarities, which all of them would have to deal with.

Christie was just fifty years old. He had been born in the United States, in a small Vermont village, but had grown up in a Wisconsin wilderness, where the Church had not yet penetrated. Thus, it happened, that he did not attend Mass, or make his first Holy Communion until he was twenty years old.

Among other trivia that surfaced, was his insistence on being addressed as "Your Grace" which was a customary form of salutation for English prelates. This appeared to be an affectation, an innocent vanity, perhaps, but it was not regarded as a good omen by some of the old guard among the clergy.

Archbishop Alexander Christie — responsible for development of new facility on Levi Anderson property.

The appearance of Christie was not reassuring to others. He looked and walked like an aristocrat. With his head high and his faded steely blue eyes under bushy eyebrows, he looked down his long nose in a superior manner, seeing more, it seems, than anyone else. He was also tall enough to dominate most crowds. Some of his priests said he was "democratic;" there were those close to him who also said he carried his chancery in his pocket, meaning that he was not long on formalities.

Among his critics, of course, were Father Heinrich and Schell, who made little effort to conceal their differences. Heinrich departed from St. Mary's Home on August 16, 1900, one day after the Archbishop's traditional visit to the motherhouse for the vow ceremony. This suggests something more than a commonplace resignation, as reported by the press. There is an insolvable mystery about this, but one must give Heinrich the benefit of the doubt. Both he and Schell, after their stormy confrontation with Christie, died in the good graces of the church.

Reorganization of St. Mary's Home

To replace Heinrich, the Archbishop assigned Father Dominic Faber, pastor of the church at St. Paul on the Willamette, as an interim superintendent. The Sisters could not have been more pleased.

Faber was the first priest the founding Sisters had met in Oregon. By pure chance he was in the railway station in Portland on July 31, 1884, when they were waiting for the train to take them to Scio near their new home in Jordan. Faber saw them there, a little group of nuns heavily draped in black, huddled in a corner, whispering to one another in German and casting furtive glances in all directions, obviously frightened by the commotion around them. They recognized him as a priest and explained, upon request, the object of their journey. Faber was most compassionate, showed them where the cathedral was a few blocks away, and promised that he would come to visit them.[2] Even Father Werner could not have been more helpful.

Faber had been born in Bavaria and like Seghers, Heinrich and others, he had come to Oregon from the North American College at Louvain. He was about forty-four in years at this time, a veteran of long pastorates all over Oregon, but mostly in the Willamette valley at Gervais and St. Paul.

Girls Move to St. Paul

In retrospect, it appears that Christie assigned him to St. Mary's Home, while remaining as pastor of St. Paul, for two reasons: first to reassure the Sisters of his support, because rumors abounded that he intended to suppress the congregation, and, secondly, to reorganize the orphan program for the Archdiocese.[3]

It was obvious that St. Mary's suffered under several burdens. Lacking adequate financial support, it was constantly threatened with something like famine. It was neither designed for nor was capable of providing adequate care of children under six. Worst of all, it was over crowded. The Archbishop was determined to remedy all three of these problems, and while he probed for solutions to the first, he initiated a program to resolve the other two.

This involved Faber from the beginning, since it was through Faber that the Archdiocese had acquired, in the spring of 1900, "a well furnished, roomy building at St. Paul."[4] The work of remodeling this proceeded rapidly under his vigilant eye so that the girls, seven years and older, were able to occupy their new residence during the same summer. It was noted then that a total of 127 girls had lived at St. Mary's Home between 1891 and 1900, some of them for three or more years.

The new residence on two acres of land only five blocks from the church, was able to accommodate fifty girls. The Sisters of the Holy Names, who had conducted an academy at St. Paul since 1861, were in charge. Christie had made arrangements with them for the girls' attendance at the academy as day students, so the new Home began under "ideal circumstances."

Unfortunately, disaster struck within a year. On the evening of July 31, 1901, the Archbishop received the following message from St. Paul: "The orphan's Home was destroyed by fire between four and six P.M. The fire originated from a defective flu in the laundry; children all safe."

"That night," the Sister diarist wrote in the St. Paul Chronicle, "the little ones slept as happily as any previous ones. The Sisters of the Holy Names offered their academy as a substitute for the ruined Home, an offer which our Most Reverend Archbishop most gratefully accepted."[5]

Meanwhile, the children of six years and under were placed with the Sisters of the Good Shepherd at Park Place near Oregon City.

About two years later, in the spring of 1903, these Sisters moved into a new convent in Portland and the Sisters of Mercy established St. Agnes Baby Home in the same building in Park Place.

This for the time being at least, resolved the most urgent of the three crises at St. Mary's Home.

The final and chronic problem was lack of money. This would never go away, though some relief eventually arrived in the form of state support. An official account of this first appeared in 1927 in a brief history of St. Mary's.

> *It is worthy of note that during this period of [ten] years intervening between 1891 and 1900, St. Mary's Home received absolutely no State aid, but depended solely for its support on the produce of the farm,and such help as was extended by charitable persons. In 1900, largely through the efforts of the late Hubert Bernards in the House, and Dr. Andrew C. Smith in the Senate, the Oregon Legislature appropriated four dollars per month, per capita, for the homeless boys. Later, this amount was increased to eight dollars per month, and finally, in 1920, the Legislature appropriated the some of sixteen dollars per month per capita for the orphan homeless, and abandoned boys* . . . .[6]

Additional support from the State and charitable agencies like United Way, arrived in the course of time. There was never enough from these sources, however, to pay the full costs. The Home has always been dependent upon private and corporate charity for a considerable portion of its budget.

A New Name

With the exodus of the girls, the Beaverton establishment acquired a modified name. It soon became "St. Mary's Home for Boys." This was, in a sense, discrimination in a title, perhaps even sexist, but nobody then noticed it, much less cared.

More than the name was changed. The boys, or at least all of the younger ones, were delighted to have the place to themselves, but they had not reckoned on the practical consequences. They were now assigned, among other chores, to work in the kitchen, the sewing room, and the laundry.

"For a few days it seemed quite a lark — something different from the regular routine. But soon everyone got tired of the kitchen assignment. One of the main jobs was to sweep up the floors and [another] to wash the dishes and pots at a metal sink in the corner."[7]

Work in the sewing room was even worse. When questioned, one of the boys replied "that he would rather go out and feed the pigs." The sewing room was girl's work, not a boy's. One had to be firm about distinctions like this, lest one lost his self respect.

But the girls were gone and the much admired Father Faber had departed after them. He had lived up to expectations. Under his direction adequate equipment was acquired. Permanent floors in the basement were installed, partitions, cupboards and storage space was provided. A better water supply was brought in. The laundry was properly equipped and electric lights were installed. One had to be present to realize how much difference all of this made in the lives of the Sisters, who no longer had to get up at 3:30 on Monday mornings to do the laundry.

A Succession of Superintendents

In 1901, Father Anthony Moore succeeded Faber. Moore, apparently, was not happy as superintendent, at least not like some of his gung-ho successors. He preferred parish work, so he was "promoted" to a parish in Salem in 1905, and Father James D. Murphy was formally appointed to take his place. Murphy responded by dying in a hurry, giving up the ghost cheerfully, perhaps, to be relieved of the weighty burden of superintendency.[8] He was only thirty two years old when he died and he had been a priest for only five. With heavy hearts his mourners buried him in the Sisters' cemetery, and awaited for his successor, the fifth in sequence since Fessler.

During this period of growth in the Northwest Church, reflecting natural expansion from birth and immigration, required many new parishes and Bishops were hard pressed to supply priests for them. Christie, like his suffragan bishops, appealed more earnestly for help from religious orders.

It was under these circumstances that Jesuit Father Joseph Tomkin arrived with orders from the Archbishop to wear three hats at the same time. He was pastor of Beaverton's little missionary church, which had been attached previously to Cedar Mill. Its membership consisted of approximately three hundred Catholics scattered over an area of about a five mile radius. He was chaplain of the motherhouse, which by this time numbered about sixty Sisters, and he was superintendent of the Boy's Home. He had scarcely begun to get things organized when he was replaced by another Jesuit (1908), with the obviously Irish name of Deeney.

William Deeney was thirty five years old and a native born Californian, then a more rare bird than now. But, unlike many Californians, he took to the Pacific Northwest without complaining about the rain for over twenty years. He was endowed with three hats also, and he wore them rather well. His principal hat, the Archbishop told him, was that of a pastor, so his work at the Home had to be neglected, at least to some extent, and no one regretted this more than he.

Full of zeal and enterprise, Deeney decided that the Church at Beaverton was inadequate, which it was. He started land hunting and a "building fund." A new parishioner donated a half-acre of land, the piece where the church now stands. To build up the fund, Fr. Deeney petitioned the help of dear old St. Patrick, the saint who, today at least, summons up visions of entertainment and cheer. Father Deeney had a "Benefit Entertainment with Portland Talent" on March 17, 1909, a rather bold venture with so many Germans around. If he made any money that night, after treating his imported talent to a midnight snack, you may be sure it was the quality of the show and not the predisposed high spirits of his patrons.

Money for the fund was not easy to come by, and Deeney was having more than ordinary troubles in this way. Since he made many trips on the electric train to and from Portland — often two a day — the Archbishop instructed him to apply for a pass to save expenses. The railroad declined to honor the Archbishop's request, explaining that the church at Beaverton had an income and, therefore, Father Deeney had to pay. The Archbishop's secretary, Father Thompson, retorted that Father Deeney was also chaplain at the orphanage. He further stated that a diocesan regulation required an institution to provide a buggy and feed for horses for the priest who came to say Mass, but how was Deeney to ask for this from the poor orphans? The Oregon Electric Company wanted everyone to know that they liked the orphans and did not feel like forcing the orphanage to provide Father Deeney with a buggy and feed for his horse. In short, Deeney got his pass.

The Levi Anderson Legacy

During Deeney's tenure, an event of enormous proportions in the history of the Home occurred so quietly that contemporary accounts fail to mention it. Father James Maxwell, one of Deeney's successors, reported it as follows:

> *In 1909 plans were made for the extension of the work of the orphanage, made possible by the will of the deceased Mr. and Mrs. Levi Anderson, who desired to establish an industrial and trade school for boys under the direction of the Archbishop. As a preliminary, an additional [54] acres of farm land were acquired, adjoining the orphanage property.*[9]

The Levi Anderson legacy was the response to Archbishop Gross' first public announcement in 1889 regarding the orphanage. Land for an "industrial and trade" school for the boys was provided at last, but there is considerable doubt about where this land lay or how it was acquired. Anderson property was in Clackamas and Multnomah Counties, not in Washington County, where the Home was located. Only one explanation then, is possible: the Archdiocese designated approximately three hundred acres of land west of the ten acres purchased by Gross in 1889, as "the Levi Anderson land." This requires the assumption that the chancery currently regarded the Blanchet land acquisition of 1861 as Archdiocesan, not specifically Boy's Home property. There is nothing illicit or unusual about this, since the Archdiocese, like any other benefactor, could donate whatever it decided to donate. The acceptance of the Anderson estate, however, implied certain obligations in its use. Designation of approximately three hundred acres of land as "Levi Anderson land" was partial fulfillment of this obligation. Additional steps taken by the Archdiocese to comply with the conditions of the Anderson will depended upon subsequent legal decisions made by the court at the request of Archdiocesan Counsel. These decisions were related to contemporary views regarding "industrial and trade schools."

When Gross used this phrase in 1889, few tax supported institutions of this kind existed, so public spirited citizens like the Andersons made provision for a number of private schools. In Spokane, for example, at approximately this time, Benedictine Father Barnabus Held from Mount Angel, opened his "Technical College."[10] Gradually, as this type of education escalated in complexity and cost, public schools replaced them and private support was withdrawn.

Archbishop Christie, meanwhile, followed a cautious course in the use of the newly designated Levi Anderson land. He permitted the Boys Home superintendent to improve the land, without making changes in the Home's legal structure or without additional industrial programs. The Home's current practice of training boys in domestic and farm work would have to do and final settlement would have to wait for another day.

Monsignor James Rauw Replaces Deeney

During the three years that Deeney was pastor of St. Cecelia's Parish in Beaverton,[11] it expanded so rapidly that the Archbishop considered it opportune to appoint a full time diocesan priest to replace him. This was Father J.J. Daum, Beaverton's first resident pastor. At the same time, Christie appointed Monsignor James Rauw, a devoted friend of St. Mary's, to replace Deeney as superintendent of the Boys' Home and spiritual director of the Sisters. Assigned by his provincial to St. Ignatius, a new parish in Portland, Deeney left Beaverton on August 17, 1911.

Although the Sisters regretted the loss of Deeney, they were delighted with Rauw. He was one of the few clerics in the Archdiocese who had supported them when others sought to suppress the congregation. Born at Rocherath, Rhine Province Germany, on March 24, 1854, Rauw was fifty seven in years, a priest for twenty years, and a monsignor for three. Despite chronic poor health, he held important posts in the Archdiocese, which merited for him the title Protonotary Apostolic. Parish work, which he attempted several times, proved to be too much for him.

A contemporary photograph of Rauw presents the likeness of General Ulysses Grant. His high forehead is furrowed with lines, indicating tenseness or anxiety, his eyes gaze intensely through narrow openings at history making events beyond, his cheeks and chin are buried behind a well-clipped black beard which hides his neck also and heightens the paleness of his other features.

He was a good manager, and unlike Father Deeney, who lacked time and interest, he spent most of his time at the Boys' Home. The Home needed him. Finances were a shambles. The Sisters were overworked. From 1886 to 1912 the Sisters had received no salary whatever for their labors. In 1913 the entire staff, including the superintendent, shared a salary of $50. This was increased by five dollars the following year and twenty dollars in the year after that. Thus the motherhouse was required to subsidize the Home to the extent of providing education, clothes, medical attention and everything else for its Sisters.

Rauw, who was also Vicar General of the Archdiocese during this period, did not approve of this state of affairs. One of his successors described what followed:

> *From this point* [Rauw's arrival] *dates the practical development of the Home. Always a capable administrator, Msgr. Rauw began a system of land clearing and by patient effort the unsightly rows of stumps [on the Anderson land] gave way to fields of golden grain. In [1915] a new wing was added. This wing, three stories in height, gave more room and allowed an advantageous rearrangement of the whole orphanage. It contained a chapel, classrooms and new quarters for the superintendent."* [12]

This addition, almost as large as the original building, was blessed by Archbishop Christie on January 19, 1913.

Sister Theresa and the Elm Trees

At this time the Superior of the Sisters at the Boys' Home was Sister Theresa Highberger. Under Theresa and the Monsignor, the Home enjoyed a golden age. The farm provided dairy products, meats, vegetables and fruit. The food was served German style, sauerkraut, sausage, apple kuchen, dumplings and other specialities. The boys had "lots of applesauce," and vegetables like rutabagas, carrots, beans and squash. Potatoes every day and prunes often. In the afternoons after school, a snack of kuchen and a glass of milk was always served.

Most of the Sisters at the Home were dearly loved by the boys, but Theresa was almost adored. The little ones, especially, lined up at her door every morning to show off a tiny scratch or cut. Whether they needed it or not, she put "medicine" on the wounds, and a patch too, if possible. Most of the little fellows wanted a chance to meet her and talk to her. They thought she was very beautiful.

Theresa had been the fourth Superior General of the Congregation of the Most Precious Blood from 1901 to 1907, and during that time had carried out the Archbishop's decision to change its name to "Sisters of St. Mary." She really was beautiful. She had a sweet, round face like a happy Shirley Temple. A child-like curiosity peeped through her dark eyes. Her mouth was small and refined in appearance, like pictures of her patron saint. Regarded also as beautiful by her two brothers, Joseph and Nicholas, she was surprisingly tough in spirit, indomitable when she decided upon a course of action.

After two terms as Superior General, Theresa was assigned to the Boys' Home as Superior. She succeeded Sister Johanna, one of the original foundresses of the Order, who took herself, and others, very seriously. Johanna was a "house mother" for the boys. She and Theresa sometimes went begging for surplus victuals on neighboring farms, riding in the convent's surrey. Compared to Theresa, Johanna was a large woman with searching eyes, and a cabbage-size heart. She sat stiffly in the surrey, like a duchess on parade. At times she acted foolishly, at least so the other Sisters thought, for example when she tried to provide food for all of the tramps who followed the railroad tracks in front of the Home.

Sister Mary Theresa was Superior at St. Mary's Home during the 1918 flu epidemic. Sisters of St. Mary of Oregon were responsible for the care of the children for more than 60 years.

Theresa bought a number of small elm trees from a nursery in Orenco and carefully planted a row of them along the west end of the Boys' Home to provide shade on hot summer days for the chapel and also for the boys' playground. She gave eight of these trees to Sister Juliana, the novice mistress then, to be planted by the novices along the chapel windows of the convent. The trees grew large and sturdy in the warmth of Oregon's sun, watered by its soft rains. In the tragic days ahead, they would become sad reminders for Theresa, of the happier times when she planted them.

Sickness and Death

The Golden Age was not without its sorrows. There were four epidemics in those years, bringing in their wakes sickness and death. In 1918 was the great flu epidemic. In the Boys' Home, the Sisters' Convent and Academy there were numerous victims of the worst plague in the history of the United States. The flu struck the Boys' Home particularly hard. Dormitories became hospital wards, with more than one hundred and twenty patients at one time. It was then that a dedicated young doctor, Charles Mason, first came to St. Mary's. He visited the boys twice a day, providing his services gratis to the Sisters, as well as to the boys. Theresa bore the brunt of the battle.

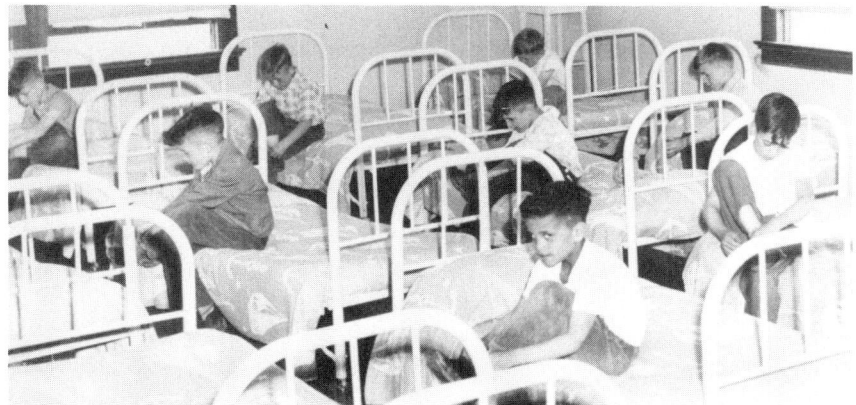

Boys' dormitory in Main Building.

> *The Superior, Sister Theresa, was on almost constant duty throughout the siege, and other sisters from the motherhouse came to assist her. The sick boys had the best of care and all but one recovered their health and strength. Twelve year old James Keegan died and was buried beneath the pine trees in the boys' lonely cemetery. Replaced as Superior, Theresa returned to the community worn out and desperately tired but ready for her assignment, which proved to be her undoing.*[13]

Death of Monsignor Rauw

The growth of the Home, its prosperity and finally, its crisis during the flu epidemic, proved to be too much for the Monsignor. Still bearing his painful burden of angina pectoris, he struggled through 1918 and entered the new year with something less than an enthusiasm for life. For several years the Archbishop had provided him with full time assistants; Father John Rubis, J.D. Neelon, Louis Derouin and Joseph Heesacker came successively to lighten his task. After the fury of the epidemic had subsided in 1919, he suffered a paralytic stroke and was forced to remain in bed. Sister Theresa became his nurse. There were no oxygen tanks then, so windows were open to the winds to provide more air for her patient, who often reported that he was "suffocating." This forced Theresa to spend long hours in the drafty, chilled air, and soon developed a severe cold, which she ignored. At last the Monsignor died, on October 24, 1919, in St. Vincent's Hospital where he had been brought before the end.

Sister Theresa by this time had acquired the dreaded disease of tuberculosis which, following the flu epidemic in Oregon, created another deadly crisis. Theresa was sure that she could be cured by rest and food "because there never had been any lung trouble in the family." To avoid spreading the disease, she built herself a little hermitage on the broad landing on the third floor fire escape of the west wing. It was a pleasant place for her bed, about which the tops of the elm trees swayed during the warm summer weather. The platform was under the striped awning and a small wooden door prevented adventurous boys from entering. Below was the boys' playground and an apple and prune orchard. When Theresa lay resting in her hermitage, she could hear the boys' laughter. They needed her love and she needed them, but the little door kept them apart.

Chapter 4

The Golden Age Continued

SISTER THERESA DIED on June 29, 1924, almost five years after the death of Monsignor Rauw. At this time, Father Joseph Heesacker was Rauw's successor as superintendent of St. Mary's. Like his two predecessors, he was a man of action, as they say now, "a shaker and a mover." He was a man of vision also, and he lasted in this demanding position of stress and physical exhaustion for eighteen years, longer than five of his predecessors put together. He left more long lasting monuments to his name, distinguished graduates as well as buildings, than any one of them.

He was thirty-four years old when he arrived at St. Mary's, a home-grown product of the valley, so to speak, since he was born into a large family in Verboort and was educated by the Sisters there for seven years, then by the Benedictines at Mount Angel. Only three days after his ordination on February 22, 1919, some months before Rauw's death, he became the assistant superintendent, actually the *de facto* boss of the works.

The first of his many projects was a gymnasium, which reveals his understanding of boys. He wrote modestly about its realization.

> *Fr. Heesacker saw the great need at St. Mary's Home for a gymnasium. This was built in 1924, and since then the athletic prowess of the boys has become history. Their scholarship has kept pace with their athletics. For six years, in taking the State*

Examinations, not one failure has been recorded. This speaks volumes for the teaching ability of the Sisters in charge of the classes.

Besides the regular eight grade course of study, the boys received instruction in dairying, agriculture, etc.[1]

Father Heesacker with 1923 championship team.
Sports is an important element of the program.

The gymnasium was an immediate success but its presence at St. Mary's raised embarrassing questions about the institutions lack of better housing. Furthermore, the old wooden buildings, by modern standards, were firetraps. State officials had called this to the attention of the superintendent and had urged the construction of permanent buildings, without, however, offering to pay for them.

The superintendent needed no prodding. He had begun to think in terms of a new campus, not on the present site, but on land acquired by the Levi Anderson legacy. This proposed new site, less than one mile west, fell within the postal district called "Huber" in honor of an early resident there. The proposal was both reasonable and timely, because of recent developments regarding the Anderson estate.

Incorporation

The originally acquired property of St. Mary's Home, the ten acres bought from Hornbuckle by Archbishop Gross, was legally entitled in the name of the Archbishop of Oregon City and was passed from one Archbishop to another in succession. In like manner, the section bought by Blanchet in 1861, part of which was designated as "Levi Anderson land," was vested in the Archbishop's name until 1920 when it was transferred to the Levi Anderson Home.

For reasons better understood by bankers and lawyers, Archbishop Christie in February, 1919, formed two corporations: St. Mary's Home, Inc., and Levi Anderson Home, Inc.[2] In the Articles of Incorporation of St. Mary's, it was explicitly stated that no assets had been transferred to that corporation. The records also stated that assets in the two corporations had come from three sources: conveyances of real property by the Archbishop; assets in the form of real property and intangibles from the Emma Anderson estate; and various gifts and bequests made by friends of the Boys Home over the years.

In a report prepared some fifty years later, the following appears:

> *On February [21], 1920, the then presiding Archbishop conveyed the eastern half of the property to St. Mary's Home and conveyed the western half of the property to Levi Anderson Home. With the exception of various easements and rights of way granted later to certain parties, the fee ownership of the property has remained in those corporate entities up to the present time. The minute books of Levi Anderson Home and St. Mary's Home indicate that on December 17, 1923, Levi Anderson Home and St. Mary's Home entered into a lease agreement whereby Levi Anderson Home would lease the real property upon which the Home was located to St. Mary's Home for the annual rent of $1,000.00. At the same time, St. Mary's Home assumed full authority to use and erect buildings and otherwise improve the Levi Anderson Home property. In 1929, that lease was renewed for the consideration of the advanced rental of $1.00 per year and is still apparently in existence.[3]*

It should be noted that the articles of St. Mary's Home were much broader than those of the Levi Anderson Home. The articles of the former had "the general object of improving and developing the condition of homeless, wayward, abandoned, neglected and abused children," while those of the latter provided "for the specific object of establishing and maintaining an institution for orphan boys." The Archbishop in forming the Levi Anderson Home, apparently intended to provide a vehicle for carrying out the purposes of the Emma Anderson will. "It can be surmised that he wished to create a corporation to assist in the operation of the Boy's Home, but which corporation could be used for other purposes in the event that the Boy's Home no longer needed assistance."

The initial officers for both corporations were Alexander Christie, President; Joseph Heesacker, Vice President; and James H. Black, Secretary. In the Minutes of the St. Mary's Corporation for August 6, 1920, the Board authorized the President "to construct additional buildings on the [St. Mary's] premises," indicating that the decision to move the campus had not yet materialized. On October 20, 1923, however, the Board authorized the President and Secretary "to borrow money and mortgage property for the construction of buildings on the corporation's premises adjacent to St. Mary's Home," that is on "Levi Anderson property." On this same day, plans and specifications for buildings were accepted. The way was now clear for Heesacker's first structure on the new campus.

For the following eight years, 1924 to 1932, the new campus was assembled piece by piece, and was occupied by the boys of St. Mary's, who scrambled to and fro in the many exchanges of quarters, happily carrying their own possessions in pillow cases.

The High School

Ground breaking on November 15, 1923, for the first of the new buildings, opened an era of clatter and traffic along the old Tualatin highway. This first unit, a residence for older boys, was finally completed in the summer of 1924 and was dedicated "with great solemnity" on September 14. It eventually acquired the title of Christie Cottage.

During this same summer "the eight grade course" was enhanced with additional grades. In the Archdiocese at this time, there were a number of Sisters' academies for girls, for example Sacred Heart at Salem, St. Mary's in downtown Portland and St. Mary's of the Valley at Beaverton. There were only two exclusively for boys, the Dominicans' Acquinas Commercial College and High School in east Portland, and the Holy Cross Fathers Columbia Prep on the west side. Both of these were relatively small and, for practical reasons, beyond the reach of boys in the Beaverton-Verboort area, where

Catholic enclaves had prospered for a half century. These were the boys that Heesacker hoped to serve.

He opened his high school in the orphanage and accepted all suitable outsiders who applied as day students. This school, never larger than sixty students at any one time, survived until 1943, when enrollment declined because of World War II. Heesacker conducted it like other Catholic boarding schools, using a lay staff to supplement the efforts of his assistant priests, whom the Archbishop supplied from time to time. The kids had inter-school competition, a drama society, year books and all the other appurtenances of contemporary high school life, which Heesacker had experienced at Mount Angel.

In 1925, at the end of the high school's first year, a second new building unit was under construction on the new site. Simply called "Main," it was dedicated during the following year. Standing near the site of the present Marian statue, it housed the administration department, the kitchen and dining rooms, the chapel, infirmary and sleeping quarters for the older boys. Other boys were housed above the "boiler room" in a separate new building, to which was added some years later, a complete laundry.

Main Building was completed in 1926.

Meanwhile, despite his renowned physical stamina, Heesacker became so exhausted that he had to take a prolonged vacation. He sat in the sun in California while Father Bernard Lee, an assistant at the Cathedral in Portland, filled in for him, serving *ad tempus* as the superintendent. Lee had the good sense to avoid starting projects of his own. He simply held the fort, as it were, awaiting Heesacker's return. When the latter returned several months later, lean and tanned, he found the President of the Board's chair empty. Archbishop Alexander Christie had gone to join his fathers in the eternal light of the next world.

The New Archbishop: Edward Daniel Howard

From his sick bed in St. Vincent's Hospital in northwest Portland, His Grace, Alexander Christie, could almost see his rising new cathedral in the crowded slope below him. His illness had been prolonged and painful, and several times during the past dozen years or so, he sought relief in the medical centers of other cities. He had come to recognize his mortality — no longer did it hold any terrors for him. When death came on April 6, 1925, it found him as ready as he would ever be.

Rome, with characteristic caution, used over one full year to replace him. On April 30, 1926, the Auxiliary Bishop of Davenport, Iowa, was appointed as the fifth Archbishop of Oregon City. Edward Daniel Howard was still young, forty-seven in years, and almost indestructible. He had lungs of leather, it was sometimes said, and when he bellowed orders, one could hear him in the next county. James Davis, his Bishop in Davenport, was recovering from a serious

Most Rev. Edward D. Howard, D.D., Fifth Archbishop of Oregon City (1926-1928), Archbishop of Portland in Oregon (1928-1966).

illness, an unhappy circumstance which delayed Howard's departure from Iowa for several weeks.

It happened, then, that Howard, who also liked to be addressed as "Your Grace," did not arrive to claim his ecclesiastical fiefdom until late August in 1926. During a speech which welcomed him, brother Bishop Edward O'Dea of Seattle tried to impress him: "The Oregon Province," O'Dea said, "is the largest in the world, and second oldest in the United States." If His Grace realized the import of these words, he did not show it. One of his greatest assets was his ability not to take things too seriously, which is why he lasted as an Archbishop for fifty years.

The Home: 1926

When he first visited the Boys' Home, the new Archbishop found a divided campus. Some of the kids were still in residence, a half-mile or more distant. The Sisters, also, lived in what was called "the Old Home," which required either a muddy or a dusty walk, depending upon the weather, from one place to the other. The bakery was the same distance from the kitchen, and other school facilities could be found in both places.

The superintendent, Howard observed, was still a young man for so much responsibility, but his age, approximately the same as many of the boys' fathers, was a fortuitous coincidence. Heesacker presented a benevolent father's image, a firm but kind man whom the boys sincerely respected. His broad forehead and receding cropped hair, gave him credibility. In his eyes there was a trace of mockery, just enough to suggest a person with a highly developed sense of humor. He wore a three-piece clerical suit with a wide collar that covered his neck and made him look like a proper seminarian. Only one of his habits was regrettable. He smoked cigarettes incessantly, lighting one after the other was gone. These and big cigars, filled the air with acrid fumes which drove away mosquitoes, but annoyed the rest of the staff.

It is not improbable that Heesacker provided the Archbishop with the following statistics for the year 1926.

> *Since its foundation, St. Mary's Home has sheltered approximately 2,000 homeless boys. Two hundred sixty nine were cared for last year (1926), eighty-five of whom were placed in*

homes or returned to relatives. Of the two hundred now at St. Mary's, ninety-five are orphaned or abandoned, and are absolutely dependent upon the Home for support; forty-eight are homeless and have one parent living who cannot make a home for them; thirty-five are wards of the Juvenile Court and thirty are classed as boarders whose parents are able to contribute something toward their support.[4]

No one, least of all the Archbishop, could dispute the superintendent's insistence that the new campus should be completed with reasonable dispatch. The depression following the end of the first World War was mostly a bad memory. It was time, certainly, to replace the crackerbox gymnasium, which was only five years old, with a larger one on the new campus. With the growth of the high school, a sport complex befitting champions was required, especially in Oregon's rainy climate. Did anyone want to exclude these kids, most of whom were classified as "disadvantaged," from the opportunities that other kids enjoyed? Certainly not. A new gymnasium, then, should be the first priority.

Another factor that had to be reckoned with, was the coach. The Home had recently employed a gifted young teacher who could squeeze impossible performances out of his meager pool of students. He did not place athletics above safety, but his teams did, and this doubtlessly softened his heart, if not his head also.

The Coach

The coach, referred to as "Professor" on all formal occasions, was James J. Robinson, a tough, charismatic Swede from Astoria. Robinson had attended Gonzaga University in Spokane. This was regarded by the kids as something very special and in their yearbooks they always called attention to it. The Sisters, too, placed Robinson on something like a pedestal, paying him the kind of respect that Knute Rockne, another Swede, received at Notre Dame.

Robinson was also "Director of Dramatics." He produced a number of plays, including one with a dangerous gorilla as the villain. This play was called "The Midnight Visitor" a "Tragi-Comedy" in two acts. You can judge the colossal nature of this production by the program, a fifty-page booklet with 119 advertisements in it including the compliments of J.K. Gill and Company and Albers Flour Mills, and polite recommendations for the purchase of Willys-Knight cars or "Famous Willamette Brand Hams, Bacons and Lard."

Also contained in the program was a list of nearly three hundred "Patrons and Patronesses," who donated cash to the cause. The list included seven priests. Conspicuous by reason of its absence, was the name of the Archbishop. Perhaps none of the kids had enough nerve to approach him.

Sister Mary Christina, bookkeeper at the Home for many years, commented in her Memoirs on another production which contained at least one adaptation often used elsewhere.

> *Professor Robinson gave many fine plays. I remember one in particular, in which one of the cast was a beautiful girl, Robert Zirkel, one of the boys whose voice had not changed yet, took the part of the girl. He came walking on the stage wearing a beautiful dress and a lovely blond girl's wig and carrying a tennis racket. After giving the play at the Home, it was given at the Aloha Hall. One of the boys in the audience admired the "girl" so much that after the show he came to meet the girl and wanted a date. Robert pulled off the wig and said, "I'm a boy!"* [5]

While these useful and entertaining stage triumphs brought a certain elegant fragrance in their wakes, the athletic triumphs of the kids got much more attention, especially among themselves. For the younger kids only, there were four teams in football, with their own league and schedule of twenty-four games, "as the means of developing future stars for the varsity." An extant photograph of these Huskies, Bears, Spartans and Trojans, presents three rows of pre-teen kids with arms folded, wearing uniforms that look more appropriate for hockey. No helmets or shoulder pads covered their muscles, just sweaters, old pants and long, heavily patched stockings. They appear to take themselves very seriously, indeed, one would judge they were about to run out to kick off for the Rose Bowl game.

There were two other levels of competitors, the Midgets who "won the only two games allotted to them on schedule," and the Varsity, a fierce looking group of only fifteen players, wearing striped sweaters and new stockings. The Coach on the upper left holds his head high, as well he might, for the "Saints" scored during that season, a total of 168 points to their opponents' 12 points.

Basketball, however, was the house speciality, focusing continued attention on the need of a replacement for the crackerbox. The St. Mary's teams performed wonders with what they had and this, too, evoked much sympathy for their needs. In the 1929 season, for example, the "Saints" played thirteen games, winning nine of them against schools many times their size, like Beaverton, whom they beat by a score of 29 to 15. These picayune scores were scarcely indicative of All American talent, but out of sixty kids in the entire school, how many basketball geniuses could one expect to find?

These customary successes seemed to inflate the boys' egos, for they now wanted to expand their exploits to other sports like tennis, golf and swimming. Some of them, it was reported, worked during the summer as caddies on an area golf course, and infected by the golf bug, they built a primitive nine-hole course in the back pasture, on which they had to avoid gopher holes and what the cows left behind.

Their swimming pool, blasted out by those who were lucky enough to avoid blowing up their own hands, was down the creek, once described as swampy and full of water tules. It was also so muddy that after someone dived in, you could not see the bottom. But it was a swimming hole, whatever its short comings, and one of the boys, carried away by adolescent dreams, described it as follows: "Nature has bountifully lavished its gifts on St. Mary's,and its most useful donation is the bubbling brook that wends its winding way

The swimming hole provides "cooling off" for hot summer days!

adjacent to the school. Last summer [1928] under skillful hands, a large space 80 by 40 feet was excavated and water from the creek was led into the pond making a glorious swimming hole." The hole would probably be condemned today, but boys in those vigorous days, usually thrived on dangerous sport just like it.

The Gymnasium

The subject of priorities was still under discussion when a fire of unknown origin destroyed the laundry and bakery in the old wooden Home. Although the main portion of the building was saved, no one overlooked the lesson which the greedy flames had taught: the old Home was still a fire trap. Being older had not made it any safer. Plans for a new residence on the Levi Anderson site received more attention and there were some who said that this should be the first and only priority until the residence was occupied.

In the end, the boys' preferences were honored. They had never abandoned their priority. They thought they could sleep in the barn if they had to, but they could not put up longer with the crackerbox. On June 12, 1930, the Board supported their position. Its members approved of the project and authorized the superintendent to borrow $25,000 for construction.

This amount would not buy a winterized doghouse today, but in 1930, when another depression was sweeping the country, $25,000 plus four times as much already in the kitty, was expected to produce a fire proof gymnasium, measuring 95 by 110 feet. One wonders about the source of the $100,000.[6] It is not improbable that it came from fire insurance on the laundry and bakery. Catholic institutions often benefited from their fires, it was one of the advantages of being Catholic. (And there were many other advantages like the weekly bingo games.)

When the gymnasium was completed in the following year, it was said to be "one of the largest in Washington County." There was no danger of inaccuracy in this statement, since the County, then, was mostly rural. Most of its barns were larger than its gymnasiums.

Not to be outclassed in his enthusiasm for the latest acquisition, one member of the Home's faculty described its impact upon the community. It soon became, he wrote, "the scene of many county-wide tournaments equipped to play on two small courts and one large playing court, volleyball facilities and punching bag equipment. Has two shower rooms, three dressing rooms and large stage and office room."[7] Easily a bargain at $125,000.

A United Campus

Heesacker's building tornado had not fizzled out when the gymnasium was occupied. On the contrary. There was still a divided campus. An addition to "Main", the administration building, had been completed by 1931, and in the following year, Heesacker Hall was built. The little boys in the first to the fifth grade, moved at last, leaving the old wooden Home to the rats. The new site was now commonly called St. Mary's High School, an oversight, perhaps, for the little fellows, but no one was interested in making a complaint.

Also left behind were the remains of two recent fires, the machine shop in which a fire had been discovered before the shop was entirely destroyed, and the dairy barn, in which the dairy herd of thirty-four cows, and the Home's four horses burned to death, along with all of the hay and feed stored there. The barn fire occurred on March 17 of this same year, just one week after the shop fire. Arson was suspected, but there was no evidence whatever to confirm it. It was quite possible, however, that the barn conflagration had been started accidentally by one or other of the boys, since experiments of various kinds were conducted in the general vicinity of the barn.

Several years later, for example, one of the older boys acquired, heaven knows how, a large steam whistle. With the aid of several adventurous companions, he rigged up a primitive steam boiler, "down by the barn," and built under it a huge fire. Soon he had enough steam to push a loaded truck over the Divide. The whistle blew madly, of course, then, suddenly, the whole contraption blew up, sending the whistle into the woods beyond. Uninjured, and very proud of themselves, the kids took to the woods also, until the coast was clear. Sometimes priests and nuns were not very understanding about such matters.

Father Heesacker's Last Years

Pranks like these robbed poor Heesacker of his youth. Somehow he had survived the worst. His health, however, was now a matter of some concern. Whether he knew it or not, his chain smoking had caught up with him and he could no longer keep up with the demands of the position he held. He realized, with some apprehension about the future, that he would have to step aside for a younger man.

As he looked around him, he could see what he had accomplished. The high school was solidly established. The coach was back. Robinson, after an absence of several years at Brophy Prep in Phoenix, had returned to St. Mary's. His being there was a comfort at a time like this. What would be the fate of the high school in the years ahead? Heesacker regarded it as his crowning achievement. What would happen to it after he departed?

Four of the school's graduates were in seminaries, studying for the priesthood. This was a sure sign that its programs were essentially academic as well as Catholic. Leo Eckstein, who had served briefly as a member of the high school faculty, had joined the Jesuits and was now at Mount St. Michael's in Spokane. Tony Gerace, a serious little fellow from Utah, would soon be ordained. Also Louis Sohler, whose father and uncle had built the new barn. Sohler, like William Delplanche, was a local boy from the upper valley, the Cornelius-Verboort area. Delplanche was older, a refugee from the wicked world. Like Gerace and Sohler, he was now studying at St. Patrick Seminary in Menlo Park, California. Both Gerace and Delplanche would be assistants to the superintendent at St. Mary's after their ordination. By that time Heesacker was gone.

On January 14, 1937, after eighteen years as superintendent, Father Joseph Heesacker spoke his goodbyes and in a flood of regrets mingled with tears, some of them his own, he drove slowly past "Main" and on to the Tualatin Valley Highway and beyond. His work at Huber was over. On arrival, he had found an orphanage in a wooden building, on departure he left an entirely new campus. He felt very tired.

His life was nearly over. The Archbishop assigned him to a small parish, St. Luke's in Woodburn, a sleepy little town then, in the Willamette Valley, south of Portland. After what was described as "a long illness," he died on January 11, 1940. His heart was still at St. Mary's and as he lay still and pale on his deathbed, in a coma from which he would never emerge, he spoke again to his boys. "Put those tools away," he would say, and sometimes he shouted, "Get in there and play ball!"

He was still the superintendent at St. Mary's.

Father James Maxwell

Heesacker's successor was Father James Maxwell who had been his assistant when he left for Woodburn.

Maxwell looked like his predecessor when he wore the customary three-piece black suit with a higher than average collar. He smiled easily, revealing a quiet sense of humor, but the lids of his eyes drooped a bit, the one on the left more than the one on the right, and this sometimes gave him a slightly cockeyed appearance. This was actually a great asset in his superiorship, since the boys dreaded nothing more than enigmatic appearances in their masters. Maxwell kept them guessing. Thus he was able to demand more with less effort. Under his administration, which lasted five years, St. Mary's became more closely identified with mainstream education.

As a priest, Maxwell also identified more actively with the clergy of the Archdiocese, and this gave him access to considerably more academic resources. It also brought greater credibility to St. Mary's. Not that it really mattered, it was no longer thought of as an orphanage.

Two years later, Maxwell could state in a public relations release, that St. Mary's staff consisted of two priests, seventeen Sisters of St. Mary of the Valley, two lay teachers, a coach, an engineer and a farm supervisor. "An enviable health record," he wrote, "has been sustained under the supervision of the medical staff, which comprises Dr. Ernest Albers, house physician; Dr. D. Stahl, dentist; and the County Health nurse, Miss Alice Robins." St. Mary's had its own dental clinic.

The high school department had an enrollment of 60 students. In the elementary department, no longer called Junior High School, as it was during the previous several years, there were 115 boys, instructed by four teachers, all of them Sisters. Total enrollment of 175 included 25 day scholars.

"The St. Mary's Home farm," Maxwell continued, "helps to provide the institution with vegetables and fruit, while the dairy furnishes milk and butter. Even some of the meats are supplied by the farm."[8]

A description of the farm, supplied some years later, could be applied here, since not much had changed.

Farm: Dairy barn, granary, potato cellar, hog house and beef cattle shed. Raise a herd of milk cattle, mostly Holstein but mixed with Jersey. Raise a herd of Polled Herefords. Chester white hogs are raised on the property. 300 acres are farmed. Raise wheat, barley, oats, spuds, vegetables of all kinds, three orchards. Farm is equipped with all modern machinery. The bigger boys help operate the farm, especially during the harvest.[9]

Photo courtesy of Oregon Historical Society No. 9668.

Vocational training provided to the boys on 300 acres of farmland.

The Vicissitudes of Richard R. Hansen

This was mostly emphasis on the positive, intended for those who supported the place. None of it lacked veracity, but there was the seamy side, which was not concealed, it was merely taken for granted. This seamy side was presented, in part, in the form of "Memories" composed for his children by Richard Hansen, an intelligent, observant lad, not unlike Lawrence Farnsworth in some respects.[10]

Hansen was one of the "bigger boys" from the day of his arrival in 1938, while Maxwell was superintendent. He wrote that he "alternatingly hated and detested" the school all during his three years there, mostly, as he candidly admitted, because of restraints on his freedom. "My father," he wrote, when he began his narrative about the Home, "had agreed to pay the school $35 per month for my board and room." Like other older boys, however, he was expected to perform various chores and to do his share of the seasonal work in the fields.

"The first few weeks at the school were not particularly enjoyable for me. I was in a new environment, surrounded by total strangers, and being sized up by all the bullies to see how far they could push me. I had several fights with other boys and in time everything worked itself out. There was a definite pecking order at the school based primarily on grade levels." The tough rules, he added, were difficult for him because in previous years he had "pretty much free roam in Washington County."

He started school as a freshman. "There were no catalogs or computer printouts listing a multitude of classes you could take. Every Freshman took the same classes. The same applied to sophomores, juniors, and seniors. I believe there was one elective, typing . . . . During the course of our stay, we had to take 2 years of Latin, a year each of algebra, geometry, business arithmetic, civics, Oregon history, and 4 years of English." Also four years of religion. The class number dropped from 23 to 3, due in part, to World War II. "Many volunteered for service as soon as war was declared. Anything to get out of the school."

There was nothing unusual about this, since it was happening in high schools all over the country.

Hansen was more attracted to farm work than he was to Latin,, "I can't say why because it was back breaking labor." Corn was a major crop, "about 100 acres and the girl's school [St. Mary's Academy] a little less." After the corn was cut it was hauled to the silos "where it was stuffed into a machine that cut it into lengths of about 1". From there it was blown up a tube and dumped into the silo . . . . The sileage had to be stamped down as it came into the silo. Two boys were generally assigned to this task. It was the worst job of the whole operation. The chopped corn just reeked. We wore boots but the juice from the chopped corn got into everything you had on. We carried the smell with us for months."

What happened after that is especially revealing.

> *Besides hay sileage was the principal feed for the cows in the winter months. As the sileage sat in the silos it gradually fermented and a heavy, syrupy fluid drained out of the silo into the pit area at the base. It was also quite hot. So hot, in fact, one couldn't put their hand a foot deep in the silo. The juice steamed as it ran out of the silo. Of course it was pure corn juice and some of the older boys figured this would be a good source for making moonshine. I don't know where they had their still or just how they went about making 'corn' from the*

THE GOLDEN AGE CONTINUED 75

Boy's enjoy working for Sister Mary Michael in convent garden, at times boys even found candy growing on the bean bushes.

Sister Mary Michael, convent gardener.

juice but they had some method figured out because they used to have some wild parties out at the pig pen.

Those naughty boys. They were also very naughty sometimes, when they gathered potatoes.

Potatoes were another crop we used to raise every year. They grew in long, straight rows a mile long. Or so it seemed. They were dug with a thing that looked like a plow with two blades except where the blades would go there were long, metal rods. This allowed some of the dirt to fall through and the potatoes to rise to the surface. The soil in which we planted and harvested potatoes was the finest of valley loam with a considerable amount of clay. Picking up potatoes in dry weather wasn't too bad a job outside of the fact it was stoop labor. But there seemed to be a coordination between the plowing up of the potatoes and the weather. When the plow started down the first row it almost always started raining. It would continue to rain until about an hour before the harvest was completed. The potatoe pickers always came in looking like they had just spent a day at the Western Front.

Picking potatoes was hard work. We had to reach out and place the potatoes in a "gunny sack" we drug along behind. When the sack was full we then tied it with binder twine and left it standing beside the row. Following along behind came the inevitable team and wagon with other boys to pick up the sacks and stack them carefully on the wagon. It didn't do to throw the sacks up on the wagon. That would bruise the potatoes and cause them to rot in storage. From there the potatoes were hauled to and stored in the "cellar" where they stayed cool and moist until needed in the kitchen.

It was also boring work. Imagine dragging a sack, sometimes weighing as much as 100 pounds around a muddy field if you can. Sometime during the late afternoon when every one was completely dog tired and worn out someone would pick up a clod thinking it was a potatoe. Seeing his mistake he would casually throw it away. Almost always it would "accidently" hit another boy working nearby. That boy would return the favor. His friend would back him up and before the foreman could get over and break up the riot everyone on the field was engaged in throwing clods, spuds, and rocks at everything that moved. I can't remember anyone ever getting seriously hurt during such a melee but there were certainly multiple bruises, black eyes, and abrasions. It was so much fun!

Many years later, Hansen could still remember significant details about the boys' religious formation though some of them were a bit confused. Since he was not a Catholic, his observations have a special value.

> *I don't recall that any effort was made to convert the protestant children while I was at St. Mary's. We all had to attend religious classes during the school year and we were required to go to mass every morning. We were offered the chance to be confirmed but no one made an issue of it. We were free to choose as we wished. To be confirmed one had to learn the catechism. I remember many of the boys dreading the day they had to take test for confirmation. Many who thought they could pass the written portion still lived in dread of the oral test which was a necessary part of the test. I can't remember anyone actually failing either of the tests but maybe some did and had to go through the procedure again. After confirmation one was then allowed to take communion and the First Communion was always a big event for the boys. They were all dressed in their Sunday best and often a visiting dignitary from the catholic hierarchy would be in attendance for the special occasion. The boys were generally given a small prayer book when the ceremony was over and many of the boys saved and cherished these small booklets the rest of their lives.*
>
> *On special feast days we had High Mass, Easter, Midnight at Christmas, All Saints Day, Palm Sunday. I recall for sure, there were probably others. The High Mass was a most impressive and moving experience. Special robes were worn, a choir was assembled, incense burned, and things dragged on for what seemed hours on end. But I did enjoy it even thought I got tired of kneeling. Unfortunately all this didn't impress me enough to become a Catholic. But it did teach me the ethics of Christian living, honesty, integrity, and the fact that there are greater powers on earth than man. For that I am grateful to the sisters and priests who labored and sacrificed so much on our behalf. I am now a confirmed and baptized Episcopalian and that, as one sister told me in later years, "is pretty close."*

During the decades that followed, Hansen successfully became a millwright, a real estate developer, a building contractor and a rare book dealer in California. He never lost his affection for some of the Sisters, particularly Sister Michael and Sister Christina, and despite some of his negative remarks in his "Memories," he really loved St. Mary's. Proof of this, I think, can be found in his enthusiasm for "reunions," which he initiated in 1978 and has continued to support with undiminished vigor ever since.

Memoirs of Sister Mary Christina

Not long after Maxwell's tenure began, Sister Christina returned to St. Mary's Home to become its bookkeeper. She had been a Sister of St. Mary of Oregon for twenty-four years, but she still retained the dove-like simplicity of a novice. She had tried her hand at teaching, putting into it her heart and soul. As some experienced judges of such matters reported, however, she was "too soft" on the children who took advantage of her. On returning to the Home, she found many surprises and savored them happily. When she wrote about them later, she still regarded them as daring adventures, even though she seldom experienced them personally.

One of her accounts is about turkeys. She could not remember whether it was the day before Thanksgiving or Christmas. The tur-

Sister Mary Christina with typing class.

keys, she said, had been delivered to the kitchen. "They had already been plucked and had been killed by being cut in the throat. Some of the other Sisters were there to help, when all of a sudden, one of the turkey's jumped up and ran down the table. The Sisters grabbed it and Sister Mary Francesca got the meat cleaver and chopped its head off."[11]

So much for the turkey. Another account concerned a poor rabbit, which fared no better although its demise was even more dramatic.

> *There was a boy by the name of Lyman Dyke who went to our high school. He used to work on weekends at St. Vincent Hospital. He must have cleaned or done something around the surgery rooms, because one day he asked some doctor if he could watch a gall bladder surgery. After the surgery, he went to Sister Agnes, who had charge of the surgery room, and asked her if she would allow him to have all the things necessary for a gall bladder surgery. He would get a little rabbit, take out its gall bladder and keep it alive. So one Saturday evening he brought home a large suitcase with all he needed and a little rabbit. Lyman lived in Christie Cottage, so he decided to have the surgery in one of the dormitories. I had charge of the cleaning of the building. I was afraid that he would get blood on the beds. He said, "No, no, no, I have the medication that will prevent blood from getting on anything." Lyman had explained to Richard Widman how to give the ether and had invited the boy who worked with him at the hospital to help with the ordeal. On Sunday morning, the three boys went to the washroom, washed very carefully to the elbows, and put on long white gowns, caps, and masks. The beds had all been shoved away and in the middle of the room was a small table with the shaved rabbit tied on it. When Richard started to give the ether, I left. I went back before dinner to find out the result of their undertaking. The rabbit was still breathing when the job was finished but died soon after that. Lyman said, "The operation was a success, but the patient died."*

"It was remarkable," Sister concluded with obvious admiration, "that high school boys could do a thing like that."

Actually, anybody could kill a rabbit, even a kid from kindergarten, though it must be admitted, finding and cutting out the gall bladder was another matter.

A last anecdote concerns Santa Claus. He did not die, but as the convent pessimist would say, "He almost died."

> At Christmas time one year, some man got the idea to entertain the boys as Santa Claus in a novel way. He rented a small airplane and painted Santa Claus Express on it. He then did a very dangerous thing. He landed on the school grounds in that small plane. One little boy said, "Oh, I didn't think there was a Santa Claus, but now I know there is. He came right down out of the sky." He gave the boys candy and little toys. When he got back into his plane, he realized he was going to have trouble getting out of there because not far from the Home there were electric wires taking power from Bonneville Dam to southern Oregon. The wires were not very high, but they were too high for him to go over. He taxied the plane as far as he could toward the power house; then he turned around and ran through the grounds and flew under those wires. Afterwards the insurance company heard about it and they said that if anything had happened to the plane or to that man, no insurance could have been collected. The following year Santa tried to drop a bag of candy and toys on the school grounds, but it landed down in the swamp. So he did not try to entertain the boys that way any more.

Aerial visit of Santa Claus.

Such charming simplicity has its own rewards. Sister Christina enjoyed a long life. She served at the Home until 1950, when superiors removed her, partly, I think, to protect her innocent naivete, which more practical people would have called gullibility. By this time, the character of the Home had changed considerably, and not all for the better. Christina was spared the sordid details.

The End of An Era

Time and worries about the declaration of war against Japan and Germany were taking their toll. Father Maxwell, when he became superintendent at St. Mary's in 1937, impressed visitors by his boyish, vigorous appearance, which sometimes confused them. Now, after five years, his face was drawn, he walked with the deliberation of a man who was not sure of himself. He worried more about money, or the lack of it, and most of all, he was anxious about the boys' future. He had grown old before his time.

The older boys recognized the change in him and when rumors surfaced that he was leaving them, they pestered him about his "new post." He chose to respond, "No Comment." They published, with his approval, a three-page mimeographed newsletter called *The Weekly Wailer,* in which they reported (in their January issue of 1942) Maxwell's forthcoming departure. They said it came "as an unexpected surprise," although they must have suspected it for some time. They sincerely regretted his leaving as "he has been a friend as well as a superintendent."

When Maxwell finally drove off five days later, "the Sisters cried" and so did many of the younger boys. But the older boys were busy winning another basketball championship, and so they soon forgot about Father Maxwell.

There is nothing more fickle than the memories of most boys.

Chapter 5

The War Years and After

FATHER ANTHONY VINCENT GERACE, at the adventurous age of fourteen, had come to St. Mary's in 1925. Small for his age and generally regarded as shy, he did not qualify for the sports which required great physical brawn and aggressive behavior, so he took refuge, as many of his kind do, in pursuits of the intellect. As a junior in high school, he starred in a stage presentation of "The Banker," in the role of a medicine man "wearing a black hat and a picturesque bow tie." His performance, a waggish classmate asserted later, was so convincing that "before the evening was over members of the audience left the hall with a few packages of medicine under [their] arms."

Sometimes boys of small stature have to prove themselves by playing the part of a more ebullient character, as Gerace did that evening of singular triumph. During the formative years which followed, he had to prove himself so often that he began to present a tougher image. Repetition seemed to create more confidence in him and he developed characteristics which he had acted out previously. When he became superintendent at the Home on January 28, 1942, just six weeks after Pearl Harbor, this rather severe personality appeared to the boys to be his real one. Some of them, at least, were in mortal fear of him and none of them dared to cross him. They respected him but respected his rigid discipline even more.

When boys appeared before him, to answer for their misdeeds, Gerace's face, already dark by nature, darkened even more. His bushy head of black hair, heavy black eyebrows and unusually small ears, gave him the appearance of a hanging judge, at least to the little kids, who were deprived of their dessert when they were found guilty. Perhaps the superintendent knew too much. As a kid at St. Mary's, he had experienced the coarseness of some and the intimidation of others. More advanced in intelligence, he knew better than they did every trick in the wiley games they played.

But Gerace was a priest and he never forgot it. Even when he waved the flag, which was most of the time, he offered a prayer for America. Patriotism drove him, and the boys through him, to extraordinary preoccupation with the war from 1942 to 1945. St. Mary's was like a military camp. A flag flapped briskly in the ocean breeze from the west. Signs with slogans like "More Scrap," "Farming for Defense," or "We Do Our Bit," were plastered all over the campus, instead of churchy exhortations to be good boys. Even the smaller kids pitched in to gather scrap metal or to cultivate Victory Gardens, which generally produced more patriotic righteousness than food.

As St. Mary's alumni became more involved in the war, Gerace promulgated a position paper for the public, as well as for his staff and students. He was very proud of the school's military records as the following illustrates.

> *The role of St. Mary's Home in the present conflict is an active and important one. Over 115 stars make up its Service Flag; of these three are gold stars.*
>
> *The boys of St. Mary's are made to feel that they constitute an integral part of the war effort, and as a result their purchases of war bonds and stamps have exceeded quotas which were thought unattainable. To serve their country in the vital production of food, the boys have been (and are) actively engaged in such types of farm work as harvesting grain and garden produce, picking fruit and nuts, caring for the dairy, making victory gardens, raising hogs, and tending to the chickens. An unusually large part of the money the boys have earned by doing this work has been used to buy additional bonds and stamps.*
>
> *The Home itself is making a substantial contribution to victory by providing a home for many children whose parents are in defense work. In line with the recommendations of the Army and Navy, the school is offering intensified instruction in the sciences, mathematics, and physical education. Such courses as*

aeronautics, chemistry, trigonometry, and mathematical analysis have been added to the curriculum to furnish the student a more technical foundation so that he can better meet present military and industrial needs.

The boys cooperate whole-heartedly in every drive, be it metal, key, or scrap. In short, they are encouraged to work, to pray, to study, to conserve.[1]

St. Mary's discipline paid off. When some of its alumni visited the Home, they had something like this to say: "We find it easy in the service because we are already regimented and are used to obeying."

Father Gerace needed no encouragement for pursuing his hard line. The soldiers and sailors were right. Whatever else St. Mary's stood for, discipline would be a priority for a long time.

Memoirs of 1942

This intense concentration on the war left many students in a quandry regarding normal activities like sports, debating and *The Weekly Wailer.* Older students began to leave soon after Gerace's arrival to "Zap the Jap!" or to vindicate their great hero, General Douglas McArthur, "one of the most brilliant strategists in history"

Rev. Anthony Gerace.

who had retreated steadily before superior Japanese forces. The yearbook was in limbo, also, first cancelled by Maxwell before his departure, then again by Gerace, who said there was not enough money to publish it.

At this point, the assistant editor of *The Weekly Wailer,* a high school junior who had practically grown up at St. Mary's, confronted Gerace to save the yearbook. This was Adam Heineman, the local entrepreneur who lacked neither imagination nor energy to carry through what he started. Eventually Adam, and several other boys, extorted a grumpy approval for publishing something akin to an annual, though officially it was called "Memoirs of 1942." Gerace expected it to be a flop. As Sister Christina tells it, however, the project was a brilliant success. Gerace lost no time in confiscating its profits.

> [Adam] went to Portland and ordered the paper, the ink, the stencils, and everything that was needed. The school colors were blue and gold, so he got blue and yellow paper and yellow tag board for the cover. Adam brought all this material home on the bus. He had to make more than one trip to have enough material for 175 books. He also bought a little Brownie camera. The boys took all the pictures they were going to put in their book, then darkened a room and developed all of them. Memoirs of 1942, St. Mary's High School, Huber, Oregon and a sketch of the Statue of Liberty were on the cover. The boys cut all the stencils, which included frames for the pictures. Harry Tobin took charge of collecting ads. Many of the boys helped him. They collected 42 ads, many from Beaverton and the others from Portland. After all the things necessary were ready, the mimeographing was done, and 29 pictures were pasted in each book. Robert Heesacker, one of the high school teachers, served as counselor for the project. The only thing they did not have done at the Home was fastening the book together. Adam took all this material in packs, ready to be stapled, and the job was done at a bookbinder in town, which included a brown piece of tape across the back, where they were stapled. I think this was a remarkable job for those boys to do, and they made $50 profit.[2]

Robert Heesacker mentioned here, was the former superintendent's nephew. As a member of the staff, he was subject to the authority of Principal Gerald B. Fahey, another Gonzaga graduate, but not a popular one like the Coach, who had become a principal elsewhere. The boys disliked Fahey. He lacked compassion and a sense of humor. He was a dour man who kept to himself, like the Irishman in one of those sad movies about Ireland. Young Heesacker filled the void left by his coldness. It would be Heesacker whom the boys at that time would remember with affection in later years, not Fahey. Not even Gerace. Richard Hansen in his "Memoirs" gives some of the reasons why.

> *I loved business arithmetic. Our teacher was a Mr. Heesacker (Bob) and he was like a father to a lot of us. I believe it was he more than anyone else in my life who helped to develop my reading habits. He would go to the library in Portland and check out a large number of books and bring them back for us to read. For some of the boys it took some force feeding but he did get them to read. All the books were good current literature, not just old, dusty classics. I especially remember Beau Geste and Lost Horizon. After reading them I was ready to go and join the Foreign Legion or to search the Himalaya Mountains for Shangra La. When possible he would take a small group of the boys on little outings. They were always educational. One time we visited the Federal Reserve Bank in Portland. One of the people there showed us a bag of nickels (5c pieces) and told us if we could pick it up and carry it to the elevator we could have it. Naturally we all tried but none could budge it, even when trying to drag it.*[3]

Many years later, Hansen could write with deep feeling: "I stopped to see him [Bob Heesacker] one time during the 2nd W[orld] W[ar] when I was on leave. He passed away a number of years ago and one of the big regrets of my life is that I didn't tell him thank you for all of the wonderful things he did for us boys at school . . . . If you can hear me now, Bob, thanks a million."

This is a tribute to Hansen as well as to Heesacker.

St. Mary's High School Is Closed

There were only three graduates on the stage that year, but the ceremony included all of the time honored customs, including the unsolicited advice of a guest speaker. Adam Heineman served as valedictorian. Since there were only two jobs for three graduates, the odd man out stoically sat through the celebration, calmly considering his grim future. His name was Dario Casale. Poor Dario. He was off to the war before the ink on his diploma was dry.

This was the next-to-last high school commencement. St. Mary's High School closed forever at the end of the 1943 school year. Day students from the neighborhood were no longer allowed to register and the few boys of high school age were bused each day to Portland's Central Catholic, which had opened in the autumn of 1939. The smaller boys, meanwhile, stayed at home to win the war by collecting junk and by buying war bonds. In one report to the Chancery on March 15, 1943, Gerace listed 38 boys with paid up bonds with a total value of $1,325.00 in addition to $393.65 in stamps for the purchase of more bonds. Presumably, this amount more than doubled before the war ended. The bonds and the stamps were theirs to do with as they pleased, a little nest egg for most, when they left the Home to enter the cruel world.

St. Mary's Boys Killed In Action

Among the alumni who served in the armed forces, more than twenty made the supreme sacrifice of their lives. Most of them had no one except their companions to mourn them, so it is especially appropriate that their names be listed here:

Glen Bayer	Bruce Gerard
Norman Blevins	Charles Holt
Jack Beste	Thomas Noud
Charles Brant	William Noud
William Brown	Ralph Pfleuger
Rev. Richard Carberry	George Sycarovich
Robert Castle	Paul Singh, Jr.
Albert Deines	Bernard Stewart
George Ezell	Harry Tobin
Robert Ezell	Jack Zirkle.
Clayton Gedding	

Two of these young men remembered the boys they left behind. Robert Castle and Harry Tobin, when they went off to battle, assigned their insurance to Father Gerace, with the instructions that "it was to be used to build a swimming pool for the boys." Some months later, Castle was shot and killed by an enemy sniper in the

South Sea Islands. When Tobin joined the navy, he requested that he be appointed to the kitchen staff on a ship, because "he did not want to kill anyone." He died in his kitchen, which the sailors called "mess." A bomb from an enemy plane had landed there in an unexpected attack, and Tobin, who would not hurt a fly, was one of the first to die.

Swimming pool built in 1949.

An Uneasy Peace

When the war was over, the nation added up its cost in terms of life and money. There was some enlightened discussion, at that time, about the impact of the war on family life, but few, if any, realized the extent of damage done to children, who are always the first victims of disaster. In care centers for children throughout the nation, subtle changes began to appear. Many children, scarred on the one hand by neglect, and on the other by permissiveness, (which had been allowed to compensate for the neglect) had become emotionally unstable. Some were violent and court records indicated that the median age of offenders of the law was slowly but inevitably dropping, warning Americans of a dangerous future ahead.

At St. Mary's, these changes began to appear as elsewhere, at first in intangible forms. Then, as time passed, they appeared more plainly. One can see in retrospect, that the war was the beginning of the end of St. Mary's as simply a residence for homeless or disadvantaged boys.

As often happens, the Sisters were the first to recognize it. Small things, like more money around. The kids could pick strawberries, raspberries and beans and earn as much in a day as they previously did in a month. One kid earned over one hundred dollars. "Imagine that, over one hundred dollars!" The boys were less docile and more independent. Nothing serious yet, but time would reveal how fast the disorder was advancing. Even the most pessimistic of the Sisters could not predict how soon it would bring them down. In less than eight years, after peace had come, they would leave St. Mary's. The changes for worse would drive them out.

Mother Mary Colette

Meanwhile, the Sisters at the Motherhouse elected a new Mother General. Sister Mary Colette, originally known as Dorothy Lorch of Portland, had been a resident pupil at the academy on the south side of the Tualatin Highway, down a ways and across from the Boy's Home. She entered the convent on September 13, 1914, and because she had special talent in music, the superior sent her to Milwaukee, Wisconsin for three years of intense studies in that demanding art. Later she attended St. Louis University on a scholarship. These relatively rare sojourns in fields afar provided her with the experience she required when, as superior general, she was required to guide her congregation through a period of dangerous change.

Even in retrospect, it is difficult to assess the administration of Mother Colette. One might simply say that she was ahead of here time, a visionary with enough strength of character and determination to force change if needed be. It was the fatal blow which led to her premature death.

Those who knew Colette well, say that she was "a snorer." Most religious communities have at least one good snorer, but not many make it to the top by becoming superior general. Doubtlessly snoring did not help Colette become superior general, but the point here is neither did it hinder her, a remarkable tribute to all concerned. For snorers, when Sisters slept in common dormitories, were not always popular with their sleeping companions.

In appearance, Colette possessed a sturdy, round face, like the typical seventh grade teacher. Her deep eyes beneath heavy brows, framed by the common kind of rimless glasses, gazed affectionately on her subjects, more like a friendly chairperson than a doting mother. Portraits of her suggest an extra chin, properly touched up, of course, but nevertheless, indisputable evidence of her daily cross, the need to diet. Having experienced the loneliness of living in the diaspora, she insisted on sending messages of cheer on all feast days to Sisters not living at the motherhouse. This kind of thoughtfulness endeared her to the troops, so to speak, but wore her out.

Her personal secretary was Sister Frances Zenner, tall and thin even in her ample robes. Frances was a music teacher, also a community mimic with a lively sense of humor. When she spoke, she seemed to be very earnest in her words and her nut-brown eyes peered steadfastly into the eyes of her listeners, confirming her transparent character and common sense mentality. She was the perfect counterpart for Colette who was the zealous prophet, burning the candle at both ends.

Colette served as Mother General for two consecutive terms, from 1948 to 1960. During the first six years she was "very popular." During the second, however, "going steadily downhill because of her dedication," who became a victim of burn-out. She kept beating a tired horse, as they say, taking No Doze pills to stay awake while she worked long hours into the night. "When she left office, she was a broken woman."[4]

While Mother Colette directed her congregation brilliantly in the bumpy years before Vatican II, she was also responsible for one serious setback during the same period. Following a bitter struggle with forces beyond her control, Colette, with the approval of her council, withdrew the Sisters of St. Mary from the Boys Home.

Fortunately, only one of the original nine foundresses was still living when this difficult decision was made. This was Sister Johanna Silbernagel. The two foundresses who died in the early years of Colette's administration, before the Home was given up, were Sister Mary Gertrude Silbernagel, Johanna's blood sister, and Mary Aloysius Bender, both of whom had lost their hearts to the Boys' Home, never to recover them.

Gertrude was the first to go. Having entered the convent at Sublimity when she was only thirteen years old, she had spent sixty two years as a member of the congregation when she died. On the evening of September 1, 1948, she suffered a severe heart attack. She was anointed, as they used to say in those days, and on the following morning about eleven o'clock, she renewed her vows in the presence of Mother Colette, then "quietly yielded up her soul to God."

When Sister Aloysius followed her in death, on December 27, 1951 after a long painful illness, only one of the foundresses remained, Johanna, the indestructible. Sister Johanna had long since retired, secure in her status as a "foundress" despite the fact, as she often complained, she had not been allowed to pronounce her religious vows with the pioneers. She kept mostly to her room, where she held court, sitting like a queen, receiving guests, to whom she offered pious platitudes when they departed. She maintained a carefully prepared list of the Sisters in the community and checked off the names of each as they appeared on feast days to offer their expressions of esteem. She dearly loved to be interviewed by reporters, and would abandon her throne at the drop of a hat to meet one in the parlor, to reminisce about the hardships of the old days.

In a way she was a complacent tyrant, demanding services like having her shoes polished and her collar starched, but her amused companions preferred to think of her as a character. She was an old lady, entitled to some eccentricities. Besides, she had long since paid her way and no one begrudged her the happiness which her grand illusions provided.

What Sister Johanna thought about the proposed withdrawal from the Boys' Home has not been recorded. The Sisters had conducted the Home for sixty-seven years, and during many of these Johanna had gone out begging from door to door to keep the place open. During the best years, there had been eighteen Sisters at work in the Home, receiving in later years only frugal salaries, precious few days off, and only rare vacations. Although they worked very hard, they had no share in making policies. The superintendent had always been a priest appointed by the Archbishop. Some of these priests, like Heesacker and Gerace, were kind to the Sisters and appreciative of what they did for the Home. But, there were a few others, before and since, who treated the Sisters in a high handed manner, exposing them to ridicule by some of the older boys.

In 1949, despite the forebodings of the prophets, all appeared to be well. Gerace reported that 201 boys were in residence that year, that a new swimming pool had been constructed and a recreation leader engaged for the summer, and that the construction of a new home for the Sisters was well under way. The total cost for operating the Home was $62,889.84 or a per diem cost per boy of $1.78, a relatively minuscule amount, thanks to the Sisters' collective annual salary of $13,500.

Sister Raphael with 17 other Sisters of St. Mary spread their loving care.

The Sister's convent, the last residence to be provided on the campus, was completed at last in the following year. Not much had been said about it, the Sisters had been living in basements for the past twenty years. The Archbishop had a sudden seizure of remorse about this and ordered special collections in all of the parishes to raise the required one hundred thousand dollars to provide a decent residence.

St. Mary's Advisory Board

What the Archbishop had accomplished for the Sisters at the Home was being accomplished in many parishes throughout the country. Teaching Sisters who had lived for decades in cramped

Convent built in 1950.

attics and cubby holes, were suddenly being provided with adequate convents with a modicum of privacy and a few creature comforts. Perhaps the shortage of nuns, who were being collectively coaxed and courted by harassed pastors for duty in the nation's burgeoning parochial schools, had something to do with this historic concession. If this was the first wave of reform in the parochial system, other waves would surely follow, almost too many of them, since most schools were eventually washed out.

For Catholic non-elementary schools, and other institutions during the same period, a different kind of reform was introduced. This was the establishment of advisory boards to share in decision making by benefactors who helped pay the bills or carried some of the burden of labor. These advisory boards were token only at first, partly because they were new and inexperienced.

Father Gerace decided to have one. The first formal meeting of this board was held at the Home on July 16, 1950. In addition to Gerace, the following were in attendance: Miss Virginia Welch, Mr. and Mrs. Edward Ebert, Mr. Henry Kropp, Mr. Alfred W. Loucks, Mrs. Kenneth Tamisie, Mr. Nelson English. English was elected chairman, Kropp Vice-Chairman, and Miss Welch, Secretary. Not that the electorate had many choices. After the usual amenities of board meetings had been satisfied, if not suffered, the board members adjourned to partake of a luncheon served in the school library. Following this, there was an inspection of buildings on campus, then the dedication of the new convent "by the Most Reverend Archbishop."

The convent was spacious. It contained private rooms for twelve Sisters, a chapel and other facilities. The members of the board were happily impressed, and the Archbishop was properly pleased. Some of the Sisters kept to themselves the anxieties they felt about the clouds on the horizon.

Father Gerace's Departure

The dedication of the convent in effect, was Gerace's swan song. For some time he had served in a triple capacity, as pastor of two small rural parishes, North Plains and Vernonia, and Superintendent of the Home. Pastoral work appealed to him. St. Cecelia's in Beaverton had developed into a major parish, requiring a seasoned pastor, who could manage its resources and hold the line in doctrine. On August 31, 1950, the Catholic Sentinel announced that Father Gerace had been assigned to St. Cecelia's and that Father John Goodrich, his assistant, had been appointed as his successor at St. Mary's. The exchange of offices took place formally on September 5, 1950.

The Sisters of St. Mary Withdraw From the Home

During the two years that followed, less subtle changes in the resident group of boys became more visible. At first, a few delinquent boys were placed in the Home, then others, and the moral tone of the place began to deteriorate. More alarmed as the days passed, the Sisters expressed their concern to Father Goodrich, who either disbelieved what they said or disregarded it. In his comments before a Board of Advisors meeting, he disputed their opinions. The Board Secretary reported his remarks as follows:

> *Work of Home outlined by Father Goodrich. [He] made [it] clear to [the] Board that [the] Home is for Dependents, not Delinquents. [The] children come from homes which are broken; where no supervision is possible; where home surroundings are to [the] child's disadvantage. Present record shows 50 Catholic children, 54 not Catholic.*[5]

Doubtlessly intended to keep the Board members on his side, these remarks fail to address the real issue, the nature of the Home's residents, not why they are there.

Worn out with the struggle, frustrated by Goodrich's tendency to overlook some of the older boys' insolence toward them, and even threatened by the violence of some, the Sisters dispatched appropriate protests to the Archbishop. Howard candidly agreed with Mother Colette regarding the basic causes of the crisis and suggested that the Sisters should be replaced with members of one of the congregations of brothers. No brothers were available, however, and matters got steadily worse until Colette, in sheer desperation, reported the situation to Luigi Cardinal Lavitrano, Prefect of the Sacred Congregation of the Affairs of Religious at the Vatican, requesting permission to withdraw the Sisters from the Boys' Home. His Eminence responded favorably without being specific. Determined to take action, but still apprehensive regarding formalities, Mother Colette wrote as follows to Archbishop Howard on July 26, 1952:

> *Your Excellency:*
> *It is our understanding that we are obliged to give one year's notice before withdrawing our sisters from any work in the Archdiocese of Portland in Oregon. In compliance with this regulation, we wish to give notification, that due to the existing conditions at St. Mary's Home, we will not be able to supply any sisters for that place after September 1, 1953.*
> *We think you realize we have tried our best to keep up the work at St. Mary's Home, since we have often discussed this problem with you. As you are aware of the seriousness of the situation, we know you are in sympathy with our decision to withdraw our sisters.*

A week later Colette sent a long, detailed letter to Cardinal Lavitrano and a copy of it to the cardinal protector of the community. Among other comments she included the following.

> *The conditions at St. Mary's Home for Boys have not improved. Several times we have consulted His Excellency Archbishop Howard, about this problem: as it has always been our habit to make our problems known to him before writing to you. His Excellency was the first to tell me to take up the matter of St. Mary's Home with you. When I spoke to him of your advice, he agreed that St. Mary's Home should be given to a community of Brothers.*

Peter Cardinal Fumasoni-Biondi, the cardinal protector, lost no time in reassuring Colette that she had acted properly and urged her to take more forceful action at once. His letter is dated August 12, 1952.

"St. Mary's Home for Boys is not, as you say, a house of your Congregation. But since the conditions are such as are described, you are quite justified to leave the place to the care of others; no other decision would come to you from the S. Congregation. Strictly, you do not need any permission, either from Rome because it is not a religious house, or from the Archbishop. You did perfectly well in notifying the Archbishop of your intention and he will try to provide in some other way for the boys; but you withdraw the Sisters as soon as you can. I say that not in an authoritative way not having jurisdiction, but in a friendly way: the sooner the better!"

"You may do well to show this letter to His Excellency the Archbishop with my affectionate esteem."

On June 3, 1953, five Franciscan Sisters, refugees from a mission in China, arrived at the Boys' Home to replace the Sisters of St. Mary. The latter remained thirteen more days, assisting the new staff to become accustomed to their duties. With heavy hearts, they left the Home for the last time on June 16, which was St. Francis Regis day, when Catholics honored a social reformer saint, who was also kicked around before he died in a blaze of controversy.

For the Sisters, the abandonment of their first major assignment marked the end of their pioneering era. Everything was changing, but the circumstances which brought about this change were the most violent of all. Thoughts of anxiety and doubt crossed the minds of many Sisters that night, when for the first time in sixty-seven years, they were all together in the same chapel.

Chapter 6

Change of the Guard

THE FRANCISCAN SISTERS, like their predecessors at St. Mary's, had experienced stormy beginnings. Several extant manuscripts provide histories in a rather bewildering pattern, at least on first sight, mostly because the founder and foundresses approach their subjects from different points of view. Even from different countries, one needs a map to follow the holy pioneers in the Orient, hopping from one exotic place to another, just one jump ahead of the Communists, who succeeded the Japanese in making their lives more complicated.[1]

These lively exercises began in 1930 when a Franciscan Bishop, coadjutor to the Vicar Apostolic of Chang-sha in China, was appointed by Pope Pius XI to the newly created Vicariate of Heng-yang. His name, suggestive of a heavenly visitor as well as Renaissance art, was Raphael Angelo Palazzi, originally of Genoa, Italy, missionary in China since 1919, and rector most of his priestly life of a seminary for educating native priests. Palazzi had few priorities: personal holiness, conversion of China and the development of a native clergy. He pursued all three with the determination of a Novice. His dying words, spoken many years later in the old convent in Genoa, where he had entered the Franciscan Order as a postulant, were "I love China and Chinese. God, please, bless China and my dear Chinese."[2]

Bishop Palazzi was interested not only in fostering a native clergy but also a native sisterhood. Following his assignment to Heng-Yang, he took the first steps toward the establishment of "The Franciscan Missionary Sisters of the Addolorata." Later he wrote about it with singular simplicity:

"From the outset, I immediately felt the need of a new Religious Congregation for women composed of young Chinese girls who would receive a sound spiritual formation and at the same time be well instructed both in doctrine and in general studies. The purpose of this would be two fold: It would enable them to assume direction of our Catholic schools and also be ready to proceed to places some distance from the center where they could prepare the Catechumens and give religious instructions to the children of the Christians, especially the newly-converted."

"With this in mind I chose some girls from our schools, who, because of their piety and studies, gave good signs of having a religious vocation. I assembled these girls in a residence, not far from Hengchow, which seemed suitable for the purpose and where they could continue their studies and acquire the necessary religious formation. I assumed personal responsibility visiting them at least once a week, sometimes oftener, to give them short conferences on the religious life and to teach them catechism."[3]

This was only the beginning. In 1938, Palazzi made his *ad limina* visit to Rome, at that time he requested, and received, "the necessary faculties to erect a new Diocesan Congregation and to open a Noviate." In the following year, he composed "Constitutions" and on the seventh of September admitted the first five candidates to the novitiate. These were:

Sister Mary Teresa Kuo of the Child Jesus
Sister Mary Gemma Keng of the Addolorata
Sister Mary Rose Lin of the Holy Rosary
Sister Mary Clare Kuo of the Immaculate Conception
Sister Mary Agnes of the Sacred Heart.

All five completed their noviceship and pronounced the religious vows of poverty, chastity and obedience on September 22, 1940. This was the quiet, unassuming birth of the new congregation.

Its founder was cautious. He did not accept a second group until over a year had passed. On December 8, 1941, five more candidates entered the novitiate. These were:

Sister Mary Gemma Wan of Jesus
Sister Mary Josephine Cheng of the Most Blessed Sacrament
Sister Mary Cecilia Lee of the Assumption
Sister Mary Angela Lee of the Immaculate
Sister Mary Catherine Ho of St. Margaret.

These new recruits were professed, as they used to say, on the Feast of St. Joseph, March 19, 1943. One of them, Sister Cecelia Lee is still on the job. She is the cook for the Our Lady of Peace Retreat House, which is also the Congregation's Motherhouse, up the Tualatin Highway a short stroll from the Boys Home.

The Sisters of St. Francis of the Holy Family

Meanwhile, political conditions in the Orient had become something less than stable. Japanese armies had over-run considerable portions of China, taking in its arrogant stride the mission of Chowtsun, Shantung, where nine American and six Chinese Sisters conducted a novitiate and school. These were Sisters of St. Francis of the Holy Family, a Pontifical Congregation with a Motherhouse just outside of Dubuque, Iowa. This mission in northern China had been established by the Congregation in 1931, when Archbishop Francis Beckman of Dubuque and Mother Dominica, the Mother General of the Congregation, responded to the request of the local bishop.

Until the Japanese invasion, the Chowtsun mission thrived. Then in 1943, the nine American Sisters were placed in a concentration camp, first in Wei Hsien and later in Peking, leaving the mission in the care of the Chinese Sisters, who survived "faithfully and heroically."[4]

Among the Sisters in confinement, four especially should be introduced. Sister M. Dulcissima, Mary Leola, Mary Agatha and Mary Hubertine. Leola, later the Mother General of the Franciscan Missionary Sisters, reveals the first step which led to their departure from one congregation for another.

"During Concentration days," she wrote, "Sister M. Dulcissima, our superior returned to America with one of the Sisters who was threatened with T.B. They were among those who went to America on the repatriation boat The Gripsholm. Sister M. Dulcissima never got back to China."

In Dubuque, Dulcissima found that many disturbing changes were taking place, Francis Beckman, the aging Archbishop, had been given a Coadjutor Archbishop *cum jure successionis*, Henry R. Rohlman, who favored "home missions" rather than "foreign missions." Both he and the current Mother General, Mother Ermina, wanted to recall the Dubuque Sisters from China. It was only a matter of time when they would have their way, but in the interim, they watched developments at Chowtsun and Peking very anxiously.

The war ended very abruptly and the Sisters were allowed to return to Chowtsun, but as Leola admitted, "we did have some terrifying experiences because of Communism." This is a characteristic understatement by Leola who faced adversity with calm, Germanic determination. She was a robust woman, someone described her as "stocky", a down-to-earth person with an enormous sense of God's Providence. She had great faith, and she would need it in the bizarre days that followed. Her account of the ordeal is presented here only in part.

> *In February of 1948 Chowtsun was taken by the Communists and we were forced to flee to Tsinan, the capital of Shantung. Not knowing what hardships might be in store for us, it was decided that the Sisters who were not enjoying good health return to America and that Sisters M. Agatha, Hubertine and myself remain to help to guide our five native Sisters and the eight postulants.*
>
> *In Tainan we helped the Franciscan Fathers in their missionary schools and taught English to adults after school hours to gain a livelihood.*
>
> *The day after Christmas 1948, we received the following notice, like a belt from a blue sky:*
>
> *No. 1 "His Excellency Archbishop Rohlman asked that the three American Sisters return to America and the native Sisters join some other Community in China."*
>
> *No. 2 "If this could not be done, both the American Sisters and the Chinese Sisters should join some other Community in China."*
>
> *No. 3 "If No. 1 and No. 2 were not satisfactory we could separate and form another Community."*
>
> *A note at the bottom of the page stated that we should seek advice and help from some bishop in China regarding our vows, and also stated we should send the [Chinese] postulants home.*

> *The Communists were nearing Tsinan and all the other Communities had received notice from their Motherhouse to be prepared to leave and to bring their native Sisters and Postulants with them to the Motherhouse. It was not a time for anyone to join another Community.*
>
> *We tried to explain our position by letter but the Mother General insisted on our carrying out her wishes.*
>
> *Permission was asked for Sister M. Agatha to come to America to explain what letters failed to do but it was not granted.*
>
> *Both Archbishop Jarre of Tsinan and Bishop A. Pinger of Chowtsun who was also a refugee of Tsinan, were angered at the unjust procedure of the Motherhouse. Archbishop Jarre advised us to appeal to Rome. But before we could act according to His Excellency's advice, Archbishop Riberi, Apostolic Nuncio to China had somehow been informed of our dilemma and asked Sister M. Agatha to come to Nanking China to explain. His Excellency sent Sister M. Agatha to America to the Motherhouse with a note. Sister M. Agatha was not given a hearing.*
>
> *When this had failed, the Nuncio urged a separation and set out to find a way. He recalled Bishop Palazzi's request for American Sisters to guide his young native Community at Hunan, Hengyang, China and suggested that both the American and Chinese of our Congregation join this Congregation and thus form a new Missionary Congregation.*[5]

Bishop Palazzi was overjoyed with the proposal, but he wanted reinforcements only on his own terms. "I replied," he wrote, "that I would be only too willing to accede to his (Riberti's) request. I did, however, state certain conditions and these were: they would have to enter my Diocesan Congregation, accepting its Constitutions, its habits and its Chinese customs; this meant that they would have to leave the Congregation of the Holy Family in order to become members, fully and unequivocally, in the Chinese Institute of the Franciscan Missionary Sisters of the Addolorata of Hengchow."

The Sisters were stunned. What were they to do, turn their backs on their own community or turn their backs on China, which they had come to love also? They sought the advice of Paulist Father Reginald Arliss, Director of the Regional Seminary in Heng-Yang. This is what he had to say.

"The Internuncio, who is the Pope's representative, wants you to stay [in China], the bishop wants you to stay, it's the same as if the Lord came down in this room and asked you to stay, what would you answer?"

As Hubertine observed later, "That settled the question for me." The three other Sisters agreed, so Archbishop Riberi applied to Rome for the required permissions. The Sacred Congregation of Religious on March 9, 1949, published a decree approving of the transfer of the Chinese Sisters and four American Sisters from one Congregation to another. By this decree, the Sisters joined Palazzi's Heng-Yang Community "without cessation of vows and with dispensation of the Canonical novitiate." The four American Sisters were formally listed by the bishop as follows:

Sister Agatha Pattee
Sister Dulcissima Dessel
Sister Mary Leola Pattebaum
Sister Hubertine Rempe.

When this decree arrived at Heng-Yang, none of the Sisters were there to receive it. Dulcissima and Agatha were still at the motherhouse in Dubuque, awaiting their fate. Leola, Hubertine and the Chinese Sisters, ordered by Palazzi, had fled the Communist takeover, first to Canton, then to Hong Kong and Macao, where they performed domestic work in a Franciscan seminary. Eventually the Roman documents arrived at Hong Kong and Dubuque, formally terminating the four American Sisters' membership in the Holy Family Community. The Sisters pronounced vows in accordance with their new state in life and began anew with gusto.

The break had not been easy, but it was over, and it was final. There was no looking back to Dubuque, no support from the cozy, comfortable motherhouse, no ties to the innumerable friends they had left behind.

Beginnings in California

Because of conditions in China, Dulcissima and Agatha were unable to obtain passports. They had been promised a hearty welcome in California by the Franciscan Fathers of the Santa Barbara Province, so they set out cheerfully for the west coast, where they

Mother M. Leola, O.S.F., Mother General of the Franciscan Missionary Sisters of Our Lady of Sorrows.

found employment teaching catechism in the Monterey-Fresno Diocese. Aloysius Joseph Willinger was the coadjutor bishop, then a kindly prelate, who befriended them vigorously as long as he lived.[6] "By Christmas 1949," Leola wrote, "with the help of a kind donor, they were in possession of Mountain View Summer Resort," which they converted into a retreat house. This became St. Clare's, the first motherhouse of the congregation in the United States.

In 1951, due to illness, Palazzi was forced to leave his diocese. He passed through Hong Kong on his way to Italy, and during his stay there he visited the Sisters of Macao. He was very impressed by Leola, and after his arrival in Italy, he sent a letter to the community "appointing her as the first Mother General. Mother Leola directed the Congregation in accordance with the Constitution."[7] In the following year, frustrated by problems in Macao and anxious about keeping her fragile group together, she proposed that all of the Sisters move to California. The bishop agreed. "In 1952, Sister Hubertina and I returned to the States," she wrote, "bringing with us 18 Chinese Sisters. Later one other Chinese girl joined our Community in America."

There was something ironic about this. The Sisters had been cut off from their original congregation in Dubuque to remain true to their call as missionaries in China. Now, still obedient to this call, they were cut off from China also. If Palazzi saw the irony in this, he did not discuss it. He visited the Sisters in Santa Cruz. "I found to my great satisfaction that the Bishops in whose Dioceses they are working are very happy with them."

The last ten years of Palazzi's life were spent in retirement, in the same Franciscan house in Genoa where he had entered as a novice. Here he considered himself as one of the friars, "refusing the usual privileges, assisting at local church events, and graciously acceding to any requests for help." There is no doubt that he lived and died for the China Mission. His last recorded words were: "I love China and the people of China. God, please, bless China and my dear Chinese!" He died suddenly and unobtrusively on October 18, 1961.

For Leola and her little band of Sisters, life would never be the same.

The Call To Oregon

When Bishop Palazzi retired, he requested his Franciscan colleague, Father Alan McCoy of the Santa Barbara Province, to serve as the Sisters' director and confidante. McCoy accepted this charge with good cheer and adopted the orphan Sisters as very special favorites. Nothing was too good for them. In late December 1952, while visiting Archbishop Howard in Portland, he spoke on their behalf, explaining to the Archbishop that they needed opportunities, like conducting retreat houses for women. They did not want schools, for the present at least, since they lacked qualified teachers. They had several of these but most members of the community were Chinese. Perhaps there was a place in the Archdiocese of Portland in Oregon for the Sisters.

The Archbishop did not hesitate to agree. He would call Mother Leola at once. He telephoned her on New Year's Day from his residence in northwest Portland. Leola responded with calm deliberation, but as His Grace proceeded with the discussion she felt more light headed than she cared to admit. The Archbishop's proposal was a bit overwhelming.

He had introduced himself first, then revealed his conversation with McCoy. Father McCoy, he said, thought the Sisters would be available for staffing the Boys' Home at Huber. The Sisters who were there planned on leaving at the end of the school year. It was urgent that others be found to replace them, and if the Missionary Sisters would come, the Archdiocese would make it worth their time. Father McCoy had mentioned that they wanted a retreat house for women. Also, a novitiate. Well then, they could have the convent, recently built at the Home, for a novitiate. He would give them fifty acres of land, contiguous to the Home "as an outright gift" providing that they would remain to staff the Home "permanently."

Mother Leola thought the proposal was very generous and she said that after she placed it before her council she would give the Archbishop her answer. She was hopeful, she added cautiously, lest the opportunity be lost, a little like a sportsman landing a big fish, that the Sisters would approve and that they could meet the required deadline of June, 1953. Encouraged by the faithful navigator, Father McCoy, Leona informed the Sisters very properly and requested their honest reactions.

The Sisters, at this time, had three residences in California, at Santa Cruz, which was the temporary motherhouse and novitiate, at 2509 L Street in Sacramento, where Sister Angela Merici, recently professed in the order, directed a catechetical mission, and at Reedley, where several Sisters including Sister Mary Dulcissima, filled in as temporary teachers in the parochial school.

The Reedley Sisters did not like the proposal. Dulcissima as superior, promptly expressed the collective opinion of all, which admitted some candid advice about dependence on bishops.

> *After reading your letter about the Oregon project we were not at all enthused. The Sisters all asked me to write to you and beg you not to accept it.*
>
> *It will be a diocesan institution and that, in itself, will put us under the bishop of the diocese, and you realize, Mother, as a missionary order we must remain independent. And even if Archbishop Howard would give us the convent and property it would make us indebted to him forever . . . .*
>
> *I would like to see our main house at Sacramento, and if we cannot get a retreat house we can build up our novitiate and with it our catechetical training school for our Sisters.*[8]

Dulcissima eventually changed her mind, as did the other Sisters in Sacramento, possibly because they were outnumbered about ten to one by those favoring the project.

Mother Leola had not been intimidated. She tendered a warm reception to the Archbishop's emissaries in early January. Fathers Martin Thielen and John Larkin were charmed by what they saw and heard in Santa Cruz. Thielen, writing on January 12 for the Archbishop, invited Leola and one of her councillors to Portland, ending his brief message with a little nosegay. "Father Larkin and I," he confided, "were deeply impressed with the spirit of your Community and hope that we may soon have you among our co-workers."

Mother Leola was very pleased with her success so far.

Seeking The Answers

Sister M. Agatha, whose rejection in Dubuque had keenly sharpened her judgement, was selected by Leola to accompany her to Portland. The two of them, after Leola had dispatched word to the other Sisters that a decision would be forthcoming soon, entrained for Portland during the last week in January. Then, having espied out the land, as it were, and having heard the conditions for occupying it from the lips of the Archbishop himself, they returned to Santa Cruz with jubilation spread across their honest German faces.

Leola lost no time in conveying her thoughts to the sisterhood. She had been especially concerned about opportunities for the Sisters' continuing education. She happily discovered, she reported, that St. Mary's of the Valley Academy was just across the highway from the Home, Marylhurst College was only a few miles distant, much closer than the Dominicans' College at San Raphael from Santa Cruz, and the University of Portland was even closer than Marylhurst, less than half the distance. In the matter of Sisters' formation, she concluded, Portland was vastly superior to Santa Cruz.

The Agreement which the Archbishop proposed was more than fair, indeed it was generous. The Archdiocese agreed as follows:

> 1. *The deed to the Sisters fifty acres of property, in return for which the Sisters will accept the obligation to staff St. Mary's Home for Boys, at Huber, Oregon. The fifty acres which shall be given to the Sisters are located at the southwest corner of the tract on which St. Mary's Home is situated. Boundaries*
> *West: Huber Avenue*
> *South: Canyon Road*

>   East: Creek running thru the Home property
>   North: A line running perpendicular to Huber Avenue,
>   and enclosing, with the other boundaries, an area
>   of fifty acres.
> 2. To authorize the erection of a generalate and novitiate, and a retreat house on the property to be deeded to the Sisters, at whatever time the Sisters shall be able to undertake these projects.
> 3. To permit the use of the convent at St. Mary's Home in Huber as a general headquarters of the Sisters, until such time as the Community shall be able to erect its own generalate and novitiate.
> 4. To encourage the various works of religion undertaken by the Sisters, such as conducting retreats, teaching catechism, and parish visiting.
> 5. Not to expect or require the Community to staff parochial schools.
> 6. To recognize the missionary character of the Community, so that, when circumstances permit, the Sisters may be able to send some of their members into foreign mission fields.[9]

There were two other concessions, one about salaries, and another about conditions for terminating the agreement.

The Sisters were required to staff the Home as needed, to provide their own operating costs for the Novitiate and motherhouse, to assign a reasonable number of Sisters to maintain retreat houses, catechetical centers and so on, as the congregation increased in membership, to meet professional standards required for those assigned to Archdiocesan roles, and to compensate the Archdiocese for the fifty acres of land "if at some future date the Sisters withdraw from the Home."

Even Sister M. Dulcissima was caught up in the general euphoria which followed. Her support was important. She was the epitome of propriety, the personification of Emily Post's decrees, tall, thin, polished, as neat as a French maid and as clean as a garden breeze. She instructed the novices in proper behavior, how to lower the voice, how to walk with dignity and as silently as a ghost or how to serve the bishop tea or coffee in the parlor. The one great mystery about her, which her novices were never able to resolve, was how she had survived as a missionary in primitive living conditions. If Leola ever knew the answer to this, she never revealed it.

The Decision

Fortunately, Leola and Agatha learned very little about Oregon's rain and the mud around the Home during the rainy season, and the dark woods beyond the barn, which looked desolate when the skies dripped endlessly in the months of winter. Santa Cruz had rain also, but it came all at once. There was so much of it that huge chunks of earth slid down onto the roads, blocking them sometimes for days. No one seemed to mind, after all, this was California. There would be complaints later about Oregon rains. As one of the Sisters used to say, with complacent tolerance, "Better California's sun than Oregon's rains." The Sisters were missionaries, were they not? Missionaries were expected to suffer anything at all, even death. But alas! Sometimes it was harder to live with rain than to be shot on a public square.

Like the Levi Anderson land, this would be a painful subject for years.

For the present, however, it was not a serious consideration. Leola's mind had been made up before she left Portland in January. Plans were begun in earnest to be ready for the great adventure, the emigration to Portland.

Great Expectations

In early March, 1953, Father Goodrich made public the decision of the Franciscan Missionary Sisters of Our Lady of Sorrows.

> *The new Community of Sisters [he said], will be arriving in June. If any of you know where I can get an electric stove for a reasonable price, let me know. We will have to install one in the Convent kitchen. As delighted as we are to have the new group come, their coming will be hard on the Building Fund reserve of $3800.00. The Home must build a fence in the back of the Convent as a kind of enclosure for the novices and postulants of the Order. Some remodeling will be necessary in the Convent itself for dining room facilities. I do not know what the situation is as yet about increased beds, bedding, plateware, tableware, kneeling benches.*[10]

The Board members were pleasantly gratified, if a bit bewildered about references to enclosures and postulants and more kneeling benches. Even Goodrich had problems with the enclosure. He wrote at considerable length to Mother Leola on March 20th:

> *In regard to your question about the enclosure: I had the architect out to look over the grounds. The first question that he asked was how many people will be using this enclosure. I could not answer him. He also asked does the enclosure have to be completely sealed so that no one can look through? How high does the wall have to be? Does it have to be of any special type of material? I could not answer any of those questions. We agreed on a section of the property behind and alongside the convent; we also came to agreement on the type of material to be used in the wall and the height of the wall. If I understand the entire problem correctly, the postulants and novices will be in the present convent only temporarily. The temporary phase may last two years, but actually you have in mind to build a separate building for them.*[11]

The superintendent was at his best in matters like this. He was anxious about many other details like the Sisters' dining room. Would they bring their own "plate ware, silverware, pots, pans, beds, bedding, etc.?" and would twenty pre-dieus in the chapel be enough? He needed two Sisters for the laundry. He thought there was enough work in the serving room "for three or four Sisters to keep busy." Also, he needed Sisters for prefecting the play grounds seven days a week, "Sisters sufficient in numbers so that one will not get too weary of the job." Also, the thought came to his mind, he could use a music teacher "and some one to play the organ in the chapel and possibly someone to teach the hymns to the children."

Was this all? By no means. There was the matter of cooking, the care of the milk room and the making of ice cream. Also, he had to have some house parents, only two Sisters living in each of the two cottages. What he wanted was not a corps of nuns, but a whole division, including a four star general. He was careful to add a cheery note of welcome.

> *Really, we are looking forward to your coming. The Sisters here now can leave any time after June the First, I presume. It would be helpful for your group to have the present Community around a few days to help you "break in." Your coming can be determined for the first part of June.*

> *You have planned an adequate staff, I feel sure. I am enclosing copies of the present Work Sheet and Time Schedule for the Sisters here now. From it you can see that they are crowded, too much so. If with the number of your Community we can scatter the work around more, I believe all will benefit, Sisters, Boys, and school.*

The "Work Sheet and Time Schedule" should have scared off the poor Sisters by this time, but they were in so deep they scarcely noticed it. The list of the duties of the local superior alone covered an entire page, typed single space, fifty lines of directives. For example:

> *Sister Superior*
> *In charge of the Infirmary, care of the sick*
> *Appoint boys to work charges, change charges every six weeks*
>   *Appoint boys to their places in dining room and appoint the "captain" for each table*
> *Appoint boys to their places in chapel*
> *Check in-coming and out-going mail of students. Any questionable mail is referred to the Superintendent*
> *Responsible for ordering groceries for kitchen, for buying medical supplies, buying candy for resale to students, buying school supplies for resale, buying of household supplies, thread, table cloths, drape material, knick knacks for banquets, etc; buying of supplies for boys' use: shoe polish, shoe strings, combs, tooth brushes, hair oil, etc.*
> *Periodically check on shoes that boys have and prepare them for shoe repair. Notify priests to take shoes to Beaverton.*
> *Take care of sale candy (penny candy on Tuesday and Thursday nights; nickel candy on Sunday)*
> *Postage for boys' letters and packages, etc.*

And much more. At least no one could say that the superintendent was disorganized.

Mother Leola responded gallantly. In a letter dated April 12, 1953, she reported on progress in the making of plans. Among other comments were the following.

> *As I mentioned on my first visit to Portland, the number of professed American Sisters is still very small and it was for this reason that I hesitated to take up the work at the Boy's Home. However, we have a fine group of Postulants, the greater number over thirty and all are very anxious to make the Boy's Home*

> a success. They will all help some way or other this year, and then be ready to take regular duties next year after they are professed.[12]

By mid-May, Leola had a game plan for the Sisters' migration. she looked forward, she wrote to Goodrich, "with happy anticipation." Then:

> There is no objection to having the newspapers report our arrival, or to the taking of pictures. However, I am wondering if our plan to arrive in two groups will itself spoil their story. The present arrangement is for a group of five to leave here by car June 2nd. They should arrive sometime June 3rd, and three other Sisters and I will arrive on the Shasta Daylight at 11:15 P.M. the same day — June 3rd. The larger group will not go north until about June 16th, or whatever date we find we can have the house ready for them after the Sisters now at Beaverton have left. That group, too, will be divided, some coming by car and some by train.[13]

The Exodus

The great exodus to Oregon began on June 2, 1953. The first group of five, including Sister Angela Merici, Sister Mary Anne and three postulants, Annette Jondura, Jean Grasser and Margaret McLaughlin, left Santa Cruz "at 4 A.M. to get an early start" in "a five passenger Buick sedan. Having decided to take Highway 101, 'the world-famous Redwood Highway,' they sallied forth in high spirits, which were considerably dampened after two days of adventure and arrival late at night in a heavy rainstorm." It was 11:30 P.M. when they drove into Huber. When they reached St. Mary's Home for Boys, they had to park in a pitch dark field. There the rain had come down heavily all day, and they had to trek through mud, and grass almost knee high, to get to the door."[14]

It was not a propitious beginning.

Mother Leola's journey came off well as planned. With Sister Mary Theresa and two postulants, Margaret Callahan and Geraldine Hanna, she left St. Clare's in Santa Cruz on June 3rd, and arrived at St. Mary's on June 4th before the Buick drove into "the pitch dark field." There was an appropriate welcome at the Home for both groups by the Sisters of St. Mary, who were even more relieved than the Superintendent, to see their successors on the scene. They had suffered considerably more than the public knew, not only from the Superintendent, who seems to have blamed them for many of his problems, but also from some of the older boys, who hissed obscene names at them, when they were out of the Superintendent's earshot. The new Sisters, of course, knew nothing about this, and hopefully never would. Nor did they realize yet (but some day they would) how hard it was to leave the good boys behind, especially the innocent little boys who needed their care and love.

In a way this was an illustrious day in the history of the Sisters of St. Mary in Oregon. It was a day of great suffering and humiliation, both signs of God's special predilection.

After they departed into the late afternoon gloom, the third contingent from Santa Cruz arrived. "They were greeted at the door with great joy, but this time only by [members of] their own community."

The Promised Land

The new Sisters agreed that, whatever the weather, Portland was a beautiful place. "The trip into Portland [from Huber] is as beautiful as they said it was," wrote Sister Anthony, one of the first arrivals who could not remember wet grass and mud. "The woods sort of grow up right along the highway, and the beautiful homes through there and the road twisted and turned through the canyon and then climbed up the hills surrounding the valley where it is sylvan and you can feel your ears pop; and then continued on into town. It was a beautiful ride, big-leafed maples and other deciduous trees among the evergreens. A beautiful place." On clear days, one could see Mt. Hood from the grassy field where the boys played. There it was, rising into the eastern sky, covered with snow all year long, dazzling white in the afternoon sunshine. There were green hills and mountains on all sides, and broad fertile valleys where orchards and truck gardens flourished. Flowers in profusion, rivaling the great horticultural centers of the world. Two great rivers not far distant and numerous streams,a beautiful place, indeed, and some, unlike Sister Angela Merici, who seems to have taken a dislike for Oregon, came to love it as the natives did.

Delores was assigned to mending clothes in Heesacker, "down in a small room with a sewing machine and piles and piles of clothes, helping to mend and trying to match socks by the bagfuls."

Angela, too, was assigned to Heesacker "before I became ill." She collected clothes from the boys lockers and brought them to the laundry. "There were oh! bags and bags of socks unmatched,and the poor Sisters tried to match those socks, which we found out later was a hopeless task."[15]

Angela admitted that she had "some interesting experiences at St. Mary's." She was House Mother for 48 first, second, third and fourth graders. "They were a lively bunch and it kept me jumping to keep up with their tricks. For the most part they are not orphans, but are victims of broken homes . . . . They come from an atmosphere of unrest and rejection, and so our major task is to make them feel loved and wanted without being too easy on them. It is a difficult balance to maintain."

Angela illustrated this point by her lively account of one little boy.

Little Mike by Sister M. Angela

While I was there [at St. Mary's], a little fellow named Mike arrived with a battered old suitcase. Father Goodrich brought him over to me and said: "Sister, Mike has come to live here. Will you take care of him?"

I looked down at the tiny fellow just 7 years old, and my heart went out in compassion for here indeed was one of Christ's little ones whom no one wanted. He had the blackest black eye I've ever seen, and his poor body was a mass of bruises. He could hardly see out of the black eye, but the other eye twinkled up a wondering look. I took his hand and we sat down to get acquainted. He was very much concerned about his suitcase full of new clothes, so he kept an eye on me while I marked every piece. Poor Mike never had any religious training, and when he saw a statue of St. Joseph on a table in the sewing room, he said: "Who's that guy?" I explained a little and he said, "I like him." Even after that, when he received a present, he ran to me and said, "I'll let big Joe take care of it," and he put the gift at St. Joseph's feet.

Mike gave us a good many difficult hours, but gradually we could see a faint ray of improvement. I think that our Blessed

> *Mother Mary and St. Joseph must rejoice when a lad like Mike learns to know Jesus and them.*[16]

Angela had other happy memories. "It would take volumes," she wrote, "to tell about all of the boys."

> *When I think of St. Mary's, I still see mountains of socks and overalls to be mended, 48 pairs of ears, hands, and feet to be checked after washing up at night; 48 necks and faces to be looked at, and 48 sets of teeth to be OK'ed. There were always two of us on duty at bed-time and we finally got the routine fixed into habits for them. It worked just fine until new boys entered. Shower nights twice a week were a continual adventure. One night they turned on all of the hot water by mistake and before we could do anything about it, the whole house was so full of steam that we could scarcely see each other above the sea of heads and steam below us. The situation took on almost nightmare proportions before we got it under control, and the Sister with me said, "I guess this is a taste of purgatory."*
>
> *The next morning they were all so sleepy we had a hard time getting them to Mass on time. St. Mary's has a beautiful Chapel for the boys.*

Soon after, Sister Angela departed for Sacramento where she and Sister Agatha worked in a very different kind of apostolate. She would never forget Oregon. When she became Superior General in 1969, succeeding Mother Leola, she moved the motherhouse back to Santa Cruz. Some Californians by adoption, especially if they came from Wisconsin, like Sister Angela, can never be happy anywhere else.

Chapter 7

The Painful Transition

It was generally believed that Father Goodrich was an able administrator. It was also said sometimes, that he was so devoted to his job he worried too much about losing it. This was a needless worry in fact, because Archbishop Howard had so much confidence in him that he gave him almost unlimited freedom in directing the Boys Home.

Members of the Board of Advisors agreed with the Archbishop. Not that they had any real jurisdiction over the superintendent. What they saw in Goodrich was the practical man, who knew enough about money to look for it in the most likely places. Actually, this was not a common talent in the kind of people who directed charitable institutions, those tender hearted folk who liked to spend money on the poor. One had to have a certain toughness to succeed in that murky fiscal world of social causes, of penny pinching, deficits and passing the hat. By every standard the superintendent was eminently successful. He organized all the proper committees. He even established new support organizations, like "The Marians," a kind of ladies auxiliary. He was skilled in recruiting key members of other promising organizations, like the Knights of Columbus, the Young Ladies Institute, the Ex-Newsboys Club, the Kiwanis, and many more. His own efforts, assisted by those of his innumerable associates, generated enough cash to keep the Home almost solvent.

It was even said that Goodrich had a little extra cash squirreled away in seventeen banks in the valley, for use on a rainy day.[1]

In his reports to the Board of Advisors, Goodrich was also very properly businesslike. He listed seasonal improvements with a kind of up-beat flourish, like a successful salesman who has unbounded faith in himself. Nothing was too trivial to be discussed, indeed triviality as the following confirms, was characteristic of most contemporary boards of advisors. It would be some time before these boards were trusted with the actual control of the institutions they represented.

Rev. John Goodrich. Marbles, always a competitive sport at the Home.

The Marian Statue

It was appropriate, the superintendent thought, that St. Mary's Home for Boys have some public identity with the patroness of the Home, Mary the Mother of God. In this he was not alone. Even before the arrival of the Franciscan Missionary Sisters he had proposed a project for erecting an outdoor statue of Mary. In the

Minutes of the Advisory Board Meeting for May 9, 1952, the following appears.

> *Mrs. [Edward] Eberdts informed the Board that the Catholic Daughters of America has adopted the project of purchasing a statue of Our Lady for St. Mary's, which will be placed on a pedestal in front of the school's entrance. The statue [and the] illumination of it will cost about $1800. At present $800 is in the treasury. The entire fund will be derived from the voluntary [sic] contributions of the members on a state-wide plan.*[2]

Two years later, on May 14, 1954, which was during Pope Pius XII's much publicized Marian Year, Goodrich informed the Board that money for the statue "had been donated by the Catholic Daughters." Mr. Stanton's wife, he said, had created a design for the base, and he showed this to the Board members. It would be five feet high, he explained. He would like this to be completed as soon as possible and, at the same time, a sign telling the public that this was St. Mary's Home for Boys be installed at the entrance. The latter was discussed at some length.[3]

In November of that same year, Mrs. Eberdts was present at the Board meeting to assist Father Goodrich in making a report on the statue. Mr. Ed Casey also reported progress on the lights. Actually there was no progress on either. At this rate, the statue could be dedicated, with great solemnity, some time in the early half of the 21st century. The sign would appear after that.

Another calendar year passed. The statue, Goodrich reported to the Board, was on its way. They would have to await its arrival before they could build "the platform." As for the sign, Mr. Casey made a motion that sixteen letters, at $40 each, be purchased. Mr. Casey offered to raise the required money. This motion, however, was modified and the proposed sign went back to the drawing board.

As for new business, Goodrich informed the Board that the Tualatin Valley Highway to be improved along the front of the Home, would cut fifty feet into the Home's land, taking a total of six acres. There followed a lively discussion about this because some members of the Board heard the rattle of money. Someone (the name is not recorded) timidly suggested "the possibility of taking money from the land to put it in reserve for [the] possibility of buying an institutional site somewhere else, or swapping Home's land for other land." [sic]

Giving due allowance for all of the maybes in this project, it remains as a not-so-subtle request for the consideration of change. In retrospect at least, this appears to be a radical solution for problems on the present site. Could this be the new highway? The enormous increase in the value of land? Or perhaps the inadequacy of the present buildings, which were designed for a different type of boy? There was no hint in the Minutes for the answer of these questions.

At long last, in September 1955, the statue was installed and dedicated as "Our Lady of Grace." Dennis Day, the popular tenor on the Jack Benny program, honored the event by singing several hymns. This, as Goodrich's business instincts assured him, guaranteed a large gathering of people who could admire the new sign also, when they entered the grounds and goggled at the famous singer. The "blue neon sign," reading "ST. MARY'S HOME FOR BOYS," occupied a prominent place in front of Main. It contained eighteen letters, an increase based on previous estimates, of $80 in cost. This cost increase deserved at least one half hour of the Board's consideration during a formal meeting.

No More Orphans

At this time, the Superintendent provided, for those who were interested, the following statistics regarding the profile of the Home:

Number of Boys: *112 at present [1955]*
Religion: *almost evenly divided, 50% Catholic and 50% non-Catholic*
Parents of the Boys:

Divorced	*102*
Married	*15*
Father Dead	*13*
Mother Dead	*4*
Both Parents Dead	*1*
ReMarried	*20*
Other	*5*

Financial Plan:

Full State Aid	*25%*
Partial State Aid	*40%*
No State Aid	*35%*

> *Average payment of those [parents] who contributed towards the care was $40.11 per month.*
> **Length of Stay:** *average was seven months.*[4]

These statistics reveal some painful conclusions: only one boy was a real orphan and one boy out of nine came from a home where the father was deceased. Divorced parents and step-fathers or step-mothers accounted for the vast majority of the boys. Even the superintendent had to admit that since his arrival great changes had taken place. He was willing to make some adjustments, very cautiously at first. "The school program," he reported later, "is special: boys [are] tested to find achievement level in arithmetic, language and reading. Then, [a] boy is placed at the level of operation and is advanced as he makes progress . . . Has worked very well."[5]

Another change that Goodrich accepted, also cautiously at first, was his increasing dependence upon his Board of Advisors, to whom he gradually gave more and more authority. By 1958, he began to receive from its members, some candid and very harsh criticism, especially regarding the Home's building facilities.

"As a new member of the board," wrote Dr. Joyl Dahl, "I was astounded at some of the conditions prevalent in the physical plant as such, and can only express my feelings in the superlative, such as appalling and deplorable. One's first impression, I am sure, after viewing the facilities, would be to advise a program of beginning from the ground up." Dahl conceded that "this was not a probability at the present time" because of the Home's financial position, but one must begin somewhere, he added, and the kitchen should have priority.[6]

Dahl was not alone in his assessment. The board's House Committee submitted three pages of "suggestions," involving almost every aspect of the building facilities, like doors, fire exit signs, lighting, showers, ventilation, drainage, etc. etc. The committee insisted that a plan for a new physical plant be completed "by July 1963," allowing several years for the hoped-for windfall from the sale of land.

Goodrich took the criticism in stride and talked at meetings about how much seminarians achieved during their summer's work with the boys and the possibility of a high school boys' residential program and the need for resurrecting the students' newsletter. Eventually, he got around to the subject of remodeling the kitchen. A team from the

Knights of Columbus had become very active. They were painting the interior of the buildings, as recommended by the House Committee, and were giving support to the kitchen project. They also built the popular Craft Shop, an attempt to broaden the base of student instruction.[7] The superintendent was busy gathering $600 here from a raffle and $400 there from a dinner, while, realistically, millions were needed to satisfy the legitimate demands of critics.

Interviews In the Newsletter

The boys eventually got their newsletter, which they called "St. Mary's Chimes," as doubtlessly suggested by their elders. For an early edition, they interviewed the superintendent. Goodrich responded with discreet candor, revealing for their benefit only, that his favorite food was roast beef. If nothing else did, this seemed to confirm what some board members already knew, that the superintendent could be classified as "very traditional." For the boys' benefit, also, the superintendent admitted that he had not been born in Oregon, but in Seattle some 180 miles north, that golf was his hobby and that St. John Bosco, who had dedicated his life to homeless boys, was his patron saint.[8]

Goodrich's assistant, Father Ronald Warren, was also interviewed. Warren said that he had been born in Portland, which was not very exciting, and that he enjoyed all sports, having none as his favorite. When questioned about his favorite food he replied: "All foods are my favorite." In other words, he liked to eat. This, too, contained some subtle insight about Warren's personality, but the boys were not interested in analyzing it. Their newsletter soon ran out of gas and no one seemed to miss it after it had disappeared over the hill. By this time, there was more evidence of change, not only in the worn out buildings, but more alarmingly, in the basic nature of the Home itself.

New Public Policies

For some time, it had been dependent for students on court referrals, which was in itself a signal for caution. The number of referrals was down, by something like 35%, reducing the Home's number of residents to approximately 82, while its budget was calculated on

100 or more. Mr. Richard DeCristoforo, the caseworker, offered one of the reasons for this. There were less children, he said, but more problems "because of the kind of children being served. The normal dependent child is being sent elsewhere." It was a national trend, he added, and it was not likely to go away.[9]

As the future darkened, DeCristoforo and Goodrich met with members of the Juvenile Court "to determine why their referrals had fallen off." During this discussion there was some difference of opinion expressed regarding "private therapy" meaning "private institutional care" versus "public policy," meaning counseling in the home and school with special "Visiting Teachers."

Goodrich asked his board during a subsequent session: "Are we serving the community where the need is greatest? The greatest need for care is at the High School level (14 – 16). Foster homes at this level, he insisted, were seldom successful. Members of the Board, after debating the pros and cons of a proposal for accepting "high school" boys was passed unanimously. "Who would pay for it?" Goodrich asked. No one seemed to know and the subject was tabled.

The superintendent's report for 1960 showed that the upper grades for grade school (including some boys older than fourteen years), had 60 pupils and the lower grades had only 20, totaling by some wonderful magic, 82. Of these, 47 had been committed by courts and 35 by non-public individuals.

In other categories, 23 were classified as having "Psychiatric backgrounds," and 9 as "Eneuretic," that is "bed wetters." Of the whole, 17 had been "Rejected by family," and 10 had "Rejected [their] own [families]."[10] None of this data was reassuring.

One year later, it was discovered that the applications were down by 39% from last year. This was only part of the bad news. The total enrollment of 78 included some Cuban boys placed at the Home by the United States Government.

The superintendent described their progress.

> *Presently [we] have ten boys. We recently returned three and accepted three more. They have asked us to take more but we are not considering an increase until after Christmas. The children have adapted well to the new environment and have not been any problem. The Federal Government pays us $6.00 per day. Mr. Cornely has assisted us in setting up our books as separate accounting has to be made for this program. They*

have separate bank accounts from which our per/diem cost is charged as well as clothing, etc.[11]

The Cubans, understandably, resisted integration with other students. They found English very difficult, which is not surprising, since many American kids also did. The Cubans were required to attend classes in English for three hours a day. Their teachers, the correspondent noted, hoped for improvement. It would be very surprising if they did not.

More About Boys

There was no improvement, however, in the current prospects for increased enrollment. The budget, thanks to the Cuban account, was balanced for 1961. Per diem costs were only $4.25, but the government paid $6.00 per Cuban boy. The Home was more and more dependent upon Court referrals, indicating, if further evidence was required, the need for an entirely different kind of program.

In his 1963 Fact Sheet, Goodrich provided a nice distinction. He wrote that only "Emotional problem [boys] were accepted. Not delinquents." To confirm this, he stated that,

> *"In the last 21 months:*
> *61 boys came from Court of Domestic Relations*
> *2 boys came from Public Welfare*
> *9 boys came from agencies*
> *7 boys placed directly by parents"*[12]

Evidence gleaned from various committee reports, however, indicate that "Emotional problem boys" sometimes behaved like delinquents. Some of them lied. They cheated and stole things. They vandalized property. They threatened adults with violence. They ran away when they could. Obviously this was not true of all of them, but there was a sizeable number to justify the practice of "lock-up," a form of isolation, which the Home was not permitted to use.[13] This was one dilemma; the Sisters had another.

The Franciscan Sisters' Dilemma

By this time, the Franciscan Missionary Sisters had second thoughts about their commitment. They had established their novi-

Sister M. Christine with boys at the circus.

tiate and motherhouse on the fifty acres conditionally allocated to them by the Archdiocese. They had also erected their retreat house for women, called "Our Lady of Peace" on the same property. In other words, the title to their land was contingent by contract on their continuance at the Boys Home.

Their staff at the Home had been reduced from a high of eighteen to eleven in 1964. Without them there was no hope whatever that the Home could operate on its annual income of approximately one hundred thousand dollars. The 1964 cost of operating was slightly more, $101,962.66, leaving a deficit of almost two thousand dollars. In addition to the eleven Sisters, the staff comprised "two priests, one caseworker, two men teachers, three cooks, two maintenance men, one seamstress [and] three farmers."

Happily for the Sisters, only grade school boys were in residence, though rumors abounded about the proposed change. How they would cope with older boys was a futurable, a menacing one which disturbed their equanimity when they prayed.

At present, they were so over-worked that burn-out was inevitable. As religious, they were required to spend several hours each day in customary spiritual exercises, attendance at the liturgy, prayer, spiritual reading and so on, all of which was rightly regarded as essential to their survival as religious. In addition to these, they were expected to work longer hours at the Home than anyone else, including the superintendent. For them there was no time for hobbies, especially for games of golf.

An examination of the Sisters' Weekly Work Schedule appears to be, as Dr. Dahl would have correctly stated, "appalling and deplorable." The Superior, Sister M. Joseph, was expected to spend $50^1/_2$

hours weekly on her carefully planned job, in addition to her work as Superior and time for "canning during Summer and Fall." Some of the other Sisters' schedules were as follows: Sister M. Gregory, $57^{3}/_{4}$ hours, "plus doing Home errands when others [are] not available." Sister M. Dolores, $57^{3}/_{4}$ hours including $28^{3}/_{4}$ hours teaching in class. Sister M. Michael, 50 hours "plus canning in Summer and Fall." Sister Paul, $56^{3}/_{4}$ hours, "plus canning in Summer and Fall." Sister Patrick Maureen, $54^{3}/_{4}$ hours "plus canning in Summer and Fall and taking boys to doctor and doing errands." Sister M. Josepha, $60^{1}/_{4}$ hours "plus canning in Summer and Fall." Sister M. Peter, who had drawn the most rigid schedule of all, $61^{3}/_{4}$ hours, "plus canning in the Summer and Fall and sometimes taking boys to doctor or doing Home errands."[14]

It was the "canning in Summer and Fall" which almost killed off the poor Sisters. This ran on frantically for days at a time with few opportunities to plan it. They were simply summoned when loads of fruit and vegetables suddenly appeared, then every one rushed to her station, like members of a volunteer fire department. Fortunately, they had many helpers, like the Guild ladies, another recently established auxiliary, which helped the Sisters, especially in domestic matters.

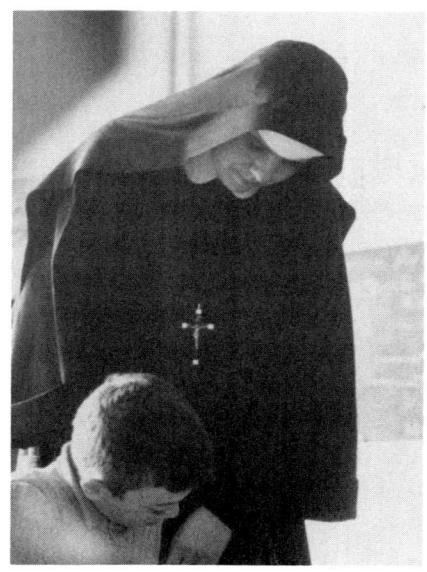

Sister M. Regina in classroom.

The Knights of Columbus

The most active of the volunteers were the Knights of Columbus, about whom the superintendent could never say enough. In his report for the board meeting on September 26, 1963, Goodrich listed some of their recent benefactors:

> *The Knights have been doing outstanding work as individual Councils. From The Dalles has come fruit (pears, peaches apples) by the truckloads. Most of the canned fruit we will have on hand will be given to us by this Council. The Albany Council sent up lumber of various kinds, toys, cases of green beans. The Eugene and Springfield Councils gave a Dodge pickup to the farm and a 1958 Edsel Station Wagon for Staff use. In addition, there were so many items that it is impossible to list them all. The Portland Council #678 has undertaken to bring a party of men out in November, January, March and May to spend the evening with all the boys in each cottage. This same Council plans to take to supper and a movie the 3 winners of the Citizenship voting each six weeks. It is also their plan to provide awards for the boys showing the most achievement in school work in January and May. Plans have also been completed to take the boys to the KOI Basketball tourney and to*

Knights of Columbus provided financial support for construction of craft shop.

> *hockey games. The North Portland Council is providing the Intramural Championship plaques and individualized plates for the winning teams in each sport. It would be safe to say that this year's schedule of participation and activity is the best thus far on the part of the Knights.*[15]

Doubtlessly gratified by this formal expression of appreciation, the Knights energetic membership picked up steam. In late 1963 they paid off the Home's deficit and bought trophies for the boys' games. That same year the State Council allocated a cash gift of $4,500, and when Goodrich announced it, he stated that the Knights had already donated services valued at $10,000. During the following year, the State Council sent another cash gift of $6,700.

High School Boys On Campus

These benefactions, which continued to arrive as long as Goodrich was in charge, doubtlessly made life more pleasant for the Sisters as well as for the boys. But problems for the Sisters continued to plague them. There was, for example, the janitor work on the campus which was not included in the schedules of assigned work. Each Sister was expected to do her share, a demand of time over and above all the rest. In the Minutes of the Sisters' Council meetings, the subject of a janitor turned up repeatedly. On August 14, 1963, the recording Sister wrote: "The problems concerning the Boys Home — namely heavy work loads for the Sisters . . . . It was decided to remind Father Goodrich about the janitor he promised to hire last June."

It was a long time before a janitor did arrive and by that time more serious difficulties had arisen. They were occasioned in part, at least, by the presence of high school boys on the campus.

From the beginning of discussions about it, the Archbishop had regarded the idea with favor. Howard had always been partial to boys. He visited St. Mary's occasionally and strolled around the grounds, talking with them and getting their views on how things ought to be done.

On May 16, 1963, Goodrich again included the high school on his agenda for the board's meeting. He suggested that the school should begin "with a nucleus of 8th graders." He also stated that "the Court [was] enthusiastic with [the proposed] program." Cost was one problem. There were others, but these were being worked out. Eight months passed. Then, on February 20, 1964, he announced that Archbishop Howard had formally approved of the project and directed that the high school should start "next year" meaning the autumn of this same year.

Elated with the best news he had received in months, Goodrich applied to the State Welfare Commission for a permit to receive at St. Mary's, boys between the ages of 6 and 17 and on March 9, 1964, he presented to the Executive Committee of the Board of Advisors, a "Certificate of Authority" from the Commission.[16]

In the Autumn of 1964, six "savable" graduates of St. Mary's grade school remained on campus. They lived in rooms in the powerhouse and traveled to school by bus, three of them to Jesuit High and three to Sunset High School.

The Ultimatum

The document which the Sisters submitted to the Superintendent contained a preamble and twelve items of contention. As one can readily observe, those presented here lack nothing by way of bite. The day of reckoning had come and St. Mary's Superintendent would not get off the hook simply by hiring a janitor.

The Preamble
Because of the physical harm that has befallen the sisters, the lack of supervision of the high school and older boys and the danger that this has put into the care of the boys the sisters find that to continue their duties at the Boy's Home will be impossible unless the following changes are put into effect by the beginning of the summer session, June 6th.

Some of the Demands
A male prefect will be on duty with the main building boys AT ALL TIMES . . . dining room, charges, [oversee all jobs] at noon, in the evenings inside and out etc. The safety of the sisters and the terrific disrespect that is now allowed to flourish demands in a sense of justice that a strong male figure be with these boys and they not be allowed to curse, threaten and mistreat the sisters.

That the promised janitorial services be provided by a hired, full time janitor who will take care of the upkeep of the main building, clean the windows, classrooms, dining rooms etc.

> *That the promised change in meals and cooks be provided. That the children's food be fixed properly, a variation in menu and appearance. That one dish meals of beans, hash, rice etc. be increased to include fresh fruit, vegetables etc. and that each meal be planned and approved by a dietitian.*
>
> *That the director will set norms of behavior for the boys in their relations to the sisters and lay staff and that these norms will be enforced. At present it is becoming a game to see who can hit a sister or at least threaten them because there is no respect given the sisters from most of the lay and priestly staff.*
>
> *That the houseparent staff be relieved of canning, that this be provided for by either buying food, having lay groups take over the chore, or hiring lay help during canning season. No sister who cans for five or six hours and runs home for noon dining room duty is going to be able to give her best to planning and carrying out cottage activities. The harm done to the children and staff by this terrific load of work in September has broken the health of sisters and has left new children lost in the midst of the time they most need a relaxed and alert houseparent.[17]*

Not all of the Sisters felt as strongly about the above as those in the motherhouse. Most of those who had survived the rigors and risks of the new order of things, did not approve of the talk about leaving the Home. They were attached to their work and believed in its effectiveness, for the most part, and as one of them said, she did not envision herself making beds at a retreat house for the rest of her life.

Thus another crisis document was composed and dispatched forthwith to long suffering Father Alan McCoy at St. Mary's Church in Stockton. Dated September 3, 1966, it concerned the "Withdrawal of our Sisters from the Boys Home." It contained four carefully typed pages with its own preamble.

> *The following is a response to the directive of August 12, 1966, received by all the houses regarding the withdrawal of our Sisters from St. Mary's Boy's Home. The undersigned Sisters who currently staff the Home do not wish to abandon this Mission. These Sisters realize the many factors and problems involved, but they would ask the council to consider the following points.*

There followed a compilation of stirring arguments for remaining at St. Mary's, including a controversial point or two: "System of working directly with the boys at all levels [is] superior to other institutions with an artificial atmosphere," and, "Not all are called to structured classroom teaching or CCD work." Another carefully worded polemic was this one: "The Home is considered a 'second-rate' mission by those who do not realize that conditions are gradually changing for better." Most boys, it was asserted, "have shown visible signs of improvement."[18]

This statement was signed by seven Sisters, among whom were six whose work schedules are described previously.

It is not likely that Mother Leola disagreed with these spiritual daughters of hers. She probably admired their spunk. She also understood the consequences of departure in terms of the Sisters' land, a touchy point raised by the seven dissenters: "By retaining the Boys Home as a mission, we will be able to keep the Retreat House Property."

This seems to have settled the matter, at least temporarily. As long as Leola was General Superior, St. Mary's would be staffed by the Franciscan Missionary Sisters.

But Leola was losing her privileged status with some of the younger American-born Sisters who had never been in China. These were now greater in number and credibility, especially since a disproportionate number of Sisters at the Home had left the community. The seven dissenters maintained that "the young Sisters" who left their ranks had been "poor risks as religious," therefore the Home had nothing to do with their departures. If the younger Sisters at Santa Cruz agreed with this, they did not give up their opposition to the Home. The attitude of some toward Oregon, expressed playfully before, now became an established principle: "We know, of course, that California's sunshine is much preferred to Oregon's rain."

These matters were commonly discussed by lay members of the staff at the Home, and sometimes the impression was given that more Sisters had left the community than actually had. Mother Leola could take some comfort by reflecting on what other religious orders were experiencing also, huge losses of membership, including much older and mature Sisters, seminarians and even priests.

It was a terrible time for religious superiors, both men and women, and bishops as well. Mother Leola lost no more than others, and much less than some.

The New Awareness

Greatly shaken by what was happening around him, the Superintendent offered the fruits of his latest cogitations to the board. He had submitted, just prior to this, a lengthy Fact Sheet to the several government agencies, which supported St. Mary's, leaning heavily in this on data supplied by his staff advisors. While he may not have liked some of the content in the report, for example the raw description of some students' behavior, he was especially pleased with the Home's affiliation with other professional organizations. They were listed as follows:

> ***Cooperative Activity with Other Agencies and Organizations:***
> *St. Mary's is a member of the National Conference of Catholic Charities; the local Catholic Charities; the Conference of Private Child Care Agencies; the Staff members belong as does the school itself, to the Child Care Association of Oregon; membership will also be taken out in the new group, Child Welfare Association of Oregon. All during the year we are working with Public Welfare County offices, County Courts, Catholic Services for Children, Psychiatric Division of the Oregon Medical School, Pacific University at Forest Grove, School of Social Service of Multnomah County.*[19]

To the board, Goodrich wrote dispiritedly: "Hopefully this year [1967] will treat me more kindly. Too many things are happening here and in the field of Social Service for us to remain unaware of the implication of these ideas and attitudes." He looked into the future and found little to comfort him.

> ***National Trends:*** *As a general statement, it may be said that all institutions have a smaller population now. The type of child coming for care is more disturbed and therefore requires more personalized care and attention. Whereas foster homes are still greatly used, this type of care is being used in great*

part for the kind of child who used to come to the institution. Nevertheless, there has been much more critical analysis of foster home care in the past two or three years by the professionals. These people have concluded that a better job must be done in this area. Children are being placed who should not be in foster homes; children are being moved from one foster home to another in defense of the system; some foster homes are not suited for this type of care. Thus, the healthy critical analysis of the program is being carried on.

Increased attention is being given to early diagnosis of emotional difficulties. Many psychiatric social workers are working in school systems. Teachers are being trained so as to detect children with emotional and characterlogical problems. This whole movement is aimed at prevention rather than allow the child to deteriorate too far.

There is still the current emphasis on "localized therapy." By this phrase is meant the tendency to leave the child in his own home, but have him tested by psychologists and/or psychiatrists and be treated by either or both. In addition, this child is placed under the supervision of the Court with the stipulation that he must see his Counsellor at regular intervals. From our own experience here we have concluded that too many such arrangements fail to accomplish their purpose. So many of our clients have been before the court repeatedly that by the time they come to us, they are quite set in their ways. But, it does seem that more recognition is being given to institutional care for the specific purpose of helping those who are disturbed or who need a "cooling off" period. A calculated guess is that the years ahead will not find a lessening of the disturbed child clientele.[20]

At last, the learned Superintendent had capitulated to the extent and complexities of the problems surrounding him. He would survive, as he fervently hoped, this new awareness, for less than a year.

Chapter 8

A Treatment Center

IN AUGUST, 1966, at the venerable age of eighty-eight, Archbishop Howard dispatched his letter of resignation to the Vatican. He was succeeded by the Bishop of Reno, where people congregated to gamble with the noisy slot machines. The new Archbishop's name was Robert J. Dwyer, a name to be reckoned with in the years that followed.

Dwyer preferred to be addressed as Your Excellency. He expected all honors due his rank and he did not approve of gambling, not even bingo, although he had built up the Reno diocese on some of the hard cash that had gone into the slot machines. He was a good business man and when he became angry, everyone knew it because his face got fiery red.

Having been born and raised in Salt Lake City, a model of civic refinement, Dwyer liked Portland, because it was respectable in appearance and because of its arty priorities. He liked beautiful things, including oil paintings and elegantly bound books. He also liked clean, orderly church buildings and rectories, with everything in spit and polish condition, with manicured lawns and shapely trees, like some of those banks and corporate headquarters.

His installation as the sixth Archbishop of Portland in Oregon took place on Monday, February 6, 1967, at St. Mary's Cathedral. If he smiled for the camera afterwards, it was not because he felt welcome. He doubtlessly felt needed, though, since it was common knowledge in the Archdiocese that its finances were in a precarious state and were getting worse every day. Portland shared this disability with many other dioceses, in part because of the on-going upheaval in the church following Vatican II. It was difficult to be a bishop then, but Dwyer liked the challenge. He was determined to hold his own against the tacky forces of radical change, and to leave the Archdiocese in a better shape than he found it.

One of his challenges was St. Mary's Home for Boys. Reports concerning this potentially volatile institution in his own backyard caused him many anxious moments. It was difficult to understand, even, what the Home was supposed to be. It had been an orphanage for many years, a residence for homeless boys, a school. It seemed to be none of these things now. Some of his priests described it as a catch-all for difficult boys who were unacceptable anywhere else. They wanted to close the place. From appearances it was obvious that it required an overhaul from the bottom up, in staff as well as in policy and physical layout.

The superintendent, the Archbishop learned, was not univocally admired, as, say, Father Gerace had been. He was too old fashioned

Archbishop Robert J. Dwyer was instrumental in changing St. Mary's to a treatment center.

and his unwillingness to recognize the trend had got the Home into its current mess. Friends said he was "traditional," using the term which was supposed to defuse the usual confrontations with the innovators. If anything, Goodrich was orthodox and he expressed it by toeing the old line, a sheep too insecure to stray or to take chances. Perhaps it was this that had blinded him so long that he had brought his institution to the brink of disaster.

Dr. Loyal Marsh

It was after Dwyer's arrival that Dr. Loyal Marsh first appeared on the scene. An alumnus of Gonzaga Prep and Gonzaga University, Marsh earned his doctorate in clinical psychology at the University of Portland. After lecturing at Creighton University and Creighton School of Medicine in Omaha for a brief period (1960-1962), he entered private practice in Portland. This academic background, it should be noted, prepared him well for the role he would soon play at St. Mary's, that is the program designer who would save the Home from total destruction, the grand architect of the new order of things.

In 1967, Richard DeCristoforo by some miraculous gift of fate, was still on the staff as caseworker. Having observed Marsh's success in restoring order to a local group home, where the boys had succeeded in sabotaging all discipline, DeCristoforo invited him to St. Mary's to make random suggestions.

"When I made my first visit," Marsh told me, resting quietly after a long day, "I observed a lot of noise; pandemonium. Teachers were screaming. Some kid was running, Dick was running after him, the kid had a knife. The place was out of control. These were not just homeless kids. These were kids who were seriously disordered, with behavior problems, from disfunctional families. This place was a depository for kids who had no other place to go."[1]

The superintendent did not welcome Marsh. It was several months before he allowed himself to be interviewed. "By that time," Marsh said, "I had a feel for the territory. The institution was falling apart and Father Goodrich knew it. He asked me to help, for example to teach the Sisters on the staff, to begin working with Dick, who was trying to maintain the kids."

Loyal Marsh, Ph.D., Associate Director.

In Praise of Goodrich

There were six Franciscan Sisters at St. Mary's, "all excellent," Marsh added, "all interested in becoming a professional corps." They were fond of the superintendent and spoke highly of him, though they realized his views on delinquent care left something to be desired. Only recently their superior had praised Goodrich highly in a letter to Santa Cruz. "Mother Gabriel," Sister M. Raymond wrote, referring to the local superior of the Sisters of the Good Shepherd, "[was] over to see Father Goodrich."

> *Although Father [Goodrich] and Mother Gabriel constantly meet in divergent views at their Catholic Charities meetings, Father gave her a most beautiful and eloquent two-hour discussion on the direction and operation of St. Mary's Home for Boys. It was certainly good for me because I had never heard him speak of his aims and principles, and coming from himself certainly corrected false interpretations both Mother Gabriel and I also had. He is extremely loyal to our Sisters and covers over their personal shortcomings and disturbances we all know so well.*[2]

The two old warriors in the battle for success agreed on one point at least.

> *[Goodrich's] conclusion was stated very emphatically: If you give me a good Religious and a highly professionalized worker — I will take the Good Religious. But if you give me a mediocre religious and a professional worker — I will take the professional worker. In this he and Mother Gabriel were both very emphatic — that before you even look at a person's qualifications, the first and most important is their religious integrity and formation.*

There was much hope for Father Goodrich, but his time had run out. He talked about his expected departure. He hoped, he said, with traces of sadness in his voice, to get a big city parish, "a plum," he called it. When he learned that the Archbishop had assigned him to the parish in Stayton, he was devastated. "He was sad," Dr. Marsh noted, careful not to overstate his diagnosis, "but obedient. Father Goodrich was a dedicated man." And an afterthought. "He had a great devotion to Mary, the Mother of God."

The New Superintendent

Thus it happened, that during the mid-summer of 1968, Goodrich's worst fears were realized. After twenty-five years at St. Mary's, he had to leave for a country parish and a young priest, his former assistant, took his much cherished place at the Home. The new priest was Father Ronald Warren, who accepted promotion gratefully, also without realizing the consequences. When questioned by a reporter from the *Valley Times*, he described his predecessor "as a giant in the field of child care."[3]

This comment said as much about Warren as it did about Goodrich. The former had unbounded faith in the efficacy of the Sacraments and God's grace, and tended to be simplistic in his theories about remedies for wayward boys, who in fact, required "treatment" by professionals. "They were just human beings with problems," he said, lightly reflecting archaic views held by many clerics. The practice of courts and welfare agencies was to put boys in home care, forcing many institutions to close. "Now they are on the streets. One kid," he added, "came from twelve different foster homes. If we got this one earlier, he would not have had so many problems."[4]

Warren, the son of a Portland police officer, "who worked extensively with youth," did not approve of Dr. Marsh's proposals. "I seldom had direct talks or transactions with him," Marsh said. Both watched anxiously as "the population fell to nearly twelve boys in Main Building at one time." The Archbishop, hastily called for an emergency meeting.

"Dwyer arrived in a mood to change the situation, Marsh recalled. "He was a good business man, able to make decisions. He wanted this meeting to decide the future of St. Mary's."

After the members of the the two boards, the Trustees and the Advisors, assembled at the Home, without Warren, who reported that he was too busy in the boys' dining room, the Archbishop gazed momentarily on those present, his face becoming very red as he reflected on the message. "Okay," he said briskly, "we are making decisions today or we are in trouble. What options do we have?"

The options were discussed, then Dwyer turned to Marsh. "What do you think we should do, Doctor?"

Marsh thought that the wisest thing to do would be to convert St. Mary's into a treatment center. The *status quo*, he said, was impossible.

"All right," Dwyer said, "St. Mary's will be a treatment center. We will develop a professional staff just like any other treatment center."[5]

With this, the historic session ended and Dwyer left the premises in his spotless, shiny car.

The Behavior Modification Program

With the assistance of DeCristoforo, Marsh had already introduced his new program which he called the "Behavior Modification Program." This was "a token economy," Marsh explained. "Points were given for positive behavior and points were deprived for negative behavior." At a subsequent meeting of both boards, he described the system more fully.

— *behave right and you earn points*
— *misbehave and the points are deducted*
— *accumulation of points allows for more privileges*

> — *increase in points moves one up on the status level, when one reaches the highest status then he is eligible to go home or to leave St. Mary's.*
> *The main concept in Behavior Modification is that you build in behavior when you knock out the bad behavior.*[6]

The system had many advantages. One of these was the absence of a painful punishment, which often created more bitterness and resentment in boys than reform. The system had a succulent carrot but no big stick. "Its emphasis," as Dr. Marsh sometimes said, "is strictly control."

Whether Marsh knew it or not, a merit program had been introduced in their colleges by sixteenth century Jesuits. It became an important element in Jesuit education and has been employed ever since. For this Jesuits have been criticized often, allegedly for something like bribing boys to study, the latter being an irreversible dogma with the so-called Progressive school in education.

But, as they say, the proof of the pudding is in the eating. Marsh's Behavior Modification Program was a dramatic success. I think it is fair to say that Dr. Marsh saved St. Mary's, first by introducing this program, and secondly, by persuading Archbishop Dwyer to change the stated function of the center from whatever it was to a treatment center. If there are some who cannot agree with this, there are others, so-called professionals, who can. These were the people who helped Marsh pick up the pieces at St. Mary's and put them back together again.

But Warren, who opposed the program, was still in charge. He was willing to step aside, however, when the Archbishop requested it. His health had deteriorated to the point of alarm. He cheerfully agreed to remain as assistant to another priest, who arrived in Portland, fresh from Reno, in December 1968.

Father Edmund Boyle

The new superintendent was Father Edmund Boyle. A streetwise native of Rhode Island with a graduate degree in social work from the University of Utah, Boyle had taken special courses in the treatment of prison populations. One might say that he was over qualified to direct a small institution like St. Mary's, with its contingent of emotionally disturbed boys. But for the Archbishop, not to mention the boys, the stakes were high, and Boyle had agreed to come in for a year or two to bail out the Home, or close it. The Archbishop had said: "Evaluate the place and examine possible uses of the facilities. Or close it." The Archbishop had also said, "I am sure that this will not be a bed of roses." Nor was it.[7]

There were six Franciscan Sisters on the staff when Boyle arrived. He wanted at least eight and began a lengthy correspondence with the new superior general, Mother M. Angela, who had moved the motherhouse back to Santa Cruz.[8] Sister M. Peter, whom Boyle called "one of the best," had been appointed "assistant director" by the Archbishop. Boyle wrote to Angela that he wanted her in another position, where she would have more influence. Angela, whose council consisted of the new generation of Sisters, responded cautiously. She kept a low profile in the give and take letters which passed between Santa Cruz and Portland, hinting at times that the Sisters would soon leave the Home. Boyle protested vigorously and urged that a new contract between the Sisters and the Archdiocese be drawn up and signed.

In all of this correspondence, Boyle referred to himself as "Director." Angela, too, had adopted a new title, "Sister President," but this innovation was short lived. Authorities in Rome disapproved and Angela became "Superior General" again. If Boyle noticed these variations, he never alluded to them. In his correspondence, he was all business, since the gravity of his situation at the Home demanded immediate and radical action.

"Father Boyle developed a good relationship with the nuns," Marsh said later, adding a nice compliment, "they were a remarkable group of ladies. They were very supportive of my efforts, they loved to learn, were very bright and good listeners. Each one furthered her own education and learned to become a professional.

"Father Boyle became a facilitator for them. He was available for counsel. The nuns had been frustrated — the community was made up of young and old. Some left the sisterhood and became paid permanent staff."[9]

The Struggle for Survival

The Sisters, however, were not Boyle's principal concern. There were almost countless other crises. The buildings were falling apart.

The lay staff was overworked and underpaid. Most of them required additional professional training. The number of boys in residence was down, and Goodrich's highly touted "care" system of a state paid per diem of $1.90 for each of only a few of the boys, fell far short of cost. Thus the financial status was desperate. A corollary was the land which had become excessively valuable and belonged legally to the Archdiocese. Should St. Mary's be moved elsewhere, on cheaper land? Or more basically, should it be terminated altogether?

Where should he begin?

He began by closing the laundry. This was not, as might appear, a trivial matter. Any change at this crucial time was regarded as a repudiation of the past. Any move could be construed as a sign of decisions to come. Boyle was in a no-win situation and he knew it.

But he had the support of Dwyer, and with some reservations, of his Board of Directors. In April of 1969, he gathered them again to make some hard decisions. They met at twelve noon and discussed his several proposals, leaving the actual decisions "for a vote at the end of the meeting." What he called "the action part of the meeting," some two hours later, "was presided over by His Excellency Archbishop Robert J. Dwyer," when the following items were put to a vote.

1. *Operate an eleven month school program, with half day sessions throughout the summer.*
2. *Close out the Farm operations and arrange to sell all livestock and equipment. Share-crop some 100 acres and at least obtain income to cover the taxes on the farm land.*
3. *Father Edmund Boyle delegated to appoint a Building Committee to decide on exact location of new Home facilities and engage Designer to initiate plans for buildings.*
4. *That Mr. Harry Kane, Father Edmund Boyle and Mr. Dudley Jones, appoint others to a Land Development Committee and immediately proceed with the plans for development of the Home property.*
5. *That the sum of ten thousand dollars be allocated from the Home funds to upgrade a Study made recently by Cornell, Howland, Hays & Merryfield, as to best use of available acreage for development.*[10]

One can be confident that this was not a rigged session, but the Archbishop's presence assured its success. The board voted favorably on all points. More significant, perhaps, is what these decisions implied, namely, the continuance of St. Mary's Home for Boys, with a new director firmly in control.

The Grand New Plan

Five days later, the results of this meeting were made public in the *Catholic Sentinel*. The banner headline stated that a "New St. Mary's Home To Be Paid By Complex." In part the article contained the following:

> *Plans for a new St. Mary's Home for Boys at Beaverton, to be financed by a self-funding process through a multi-million dollar commercial industrial development program on the institution's present acreage, have been announced by Archbishop Robert J. Dwyer.*
>
> *At a meeting of the Home's trustees and board plus the Archbishop, April 5, it was decided to go ahead with plans for construction of four residence cottages, a school a gymnasium, Sisters' convent and rectory.*
>
> *The plan includes use by St. Mary's Home for Boys of 30 to 50 acres of its present 465 acres of land. The remaining 400 plus acres will be developed as a commercial industrial complex.*
>
> *Dudley Jones of Portland has been appointed by Archbishop Dwyer to head the development program.*
>
> *"The project will be a commercial and industrial development in keeping with the growing environs of the Beaverton Area," Jones said. Definitive plans for the complex will be announced by early summer, he said.*
>
> *Father Edmund J. Boyle, director of St. Mary's Home for Boys, said plans for the new Home facilities follow modern trends in services to children, geared to group homes rather than institutional life.*
>
> *The new plant will provide group living for disturbed children, accommodating 80 boys.*
>
> *Cost of construction will not be determined until after conferences, with architects and building experts, Father Boyle said.*
>
> *Two committees will be appointed for the over all project, one for the development plan and one for construction of the new boys' Home.*
>
> *Father Boyle pointed out that the decision to rebuild the Home "is not a sudden move' but that it had been planned for*

a number of years by officials at the institution.
"But it has become more critical to make the decision now. It is necessary to do it as soon as possible," he said. "What has been good in the past at St. Mary's will be better in the future."
As new buildings are completed for use, on a nearby site, the old structures will be removed, Father Boyle said.
In present planning, Father Boyle said, the school is taking a new direction in caring for disturbed children.[11]

The cat was now out of the bag, and when those who let it go tried to put it back in, the bag had vanished.

The Results

During the lively days which followed, several committees worked feverishly to put together plans for the grand new campus. Each existing building was examined and reexamined by fire marshals, moving contractors, engineers, architects, demolition squads, bankers, politicians and sewer experts; also by several committees comprising monsignors, priests, medical doctors, psychologists, sexologists, insurance brokers, real estate executives, school officials, even some common people who rose to the occasion by keeping a lid on a very explosive barrel of profits.

The buzz word was "Rebuild." Minutes of the board meetings bubbled with effervescence, like champagne. The immediate future looked so prosperous that Dudley Jones requested all discussions to be kept confidential, though an army of interested parties already knew what was going on. Not a few of these were poised in readiness, to take advantage of land development plans. Even one of the committee members, who committed suicide later, yielded to temptation; he allowed himself to be drawn into activities that were clearly conflicts of interest.

Dr. Marsh, however, remained aloof from all the above. There was nothing confidential about his priorities and for some board members, his presentation at the scheduled meeting on September 25, 1969, was a refreshing departure from the hype about money.

Dr. Marsh [the secretary reported] presented to the Board the present school program. The past program was designed on a residential school model. The program has now moved towards the more disturbed child and as a consequence the treatment program has had to be updated. The primary model is now behavior modification aimed at changing behavior. The system of points as utilized was explained. Also, the hiring of more professional help and the utilization of community for schooling. The prime referral agents now are the Courts and Public Welfare. No boy is now accepted on a private basis. There has to be an agency involvement.[12]

At a later meeting of the board, attended by the Archbishop, Boyle announced that the Home now had a savings account of $36,916.90 and that "the population of 40 boys [would keep] the program essentially in balance for 1970."[13]

His Excellency was pleased. "We are grateful to you, Father Boyle," he said, "for the fine work you have done here at St. Mary's. Dr. Marsh, we leave the program in your hands to be carried out, knowing it is in good hands. We appreciate the help of the Advisory Board members. The program today is different from 60 to 70 years ago, when it started. There are so many who need help, and we can take care of so few. But perhaps they may be the lever. May the Lord of the harvest bless and enrich your work."[14]

Another Barn Fire

On October 5, 1969, the huge barn built by the Sohlers in the summer of 1953, burned to the ground. The spectacular fire was reported by Portland's Journal with the caption in headline type: "Boys At St. Mary's Can't Be Bothered By Fire."

> *Either the boys at St. Mary's Boys Home (west of Beaverton) are among the most sophisticated of their generation, or its soundest sleepers . . .that's the conclusion of Journal staffer Brian Bell. Bell turned out for the two-alarm blaze at the Boys Home in the wee hours of Sunday morning. Although the burning barn on the Boys Home property was a blaze to behold for miles around, the Journal staffer said he saw nary a light go on in the Home or a face in the window.*[15]

The burning of the barn happily solved one problem, but others related to the physical condition of the plant that remained. The fire marshal had condemned Main, the largest building on the campus, and much to the consternation of former students and older staff members, plans were announced that it would be razed. The ground under the swimming pool was sinking, other buildings were said to be beyond repair, though two of them, a contractor thought, were worth saving.

Boyle had his eye on the Convent. Since the number of Sisters in residence there had steadily declined, he requested those still in residence to move into the retreat house. This did not improve relations with Santa Cruz, but survival could not yet yield to sweetness and light.

Consideration of Alternate Sites

Alternate sites for a new campus were soon explored. One of these was the former Jesuit Novitiate near Sheridan, Oregon. On February 22, 1970, a committee of the Advisory Board, with Fathers Morton Park of Catholic Charities and William Hamilton, visited this facility "to evaluate it for use as a child care institution." They were somewhat awed by its great size. The committee filed a two page report, giving the pros and cons, the latter outweighing the former. "The Novitiate is 50 miles from Portland, which causes a handicap because 30% of our court committed boys are from Mult[nomah] County. This distance also makes it difficult for the staff that are attending classes in Portland. The distance makes it difficult to get the full benefit of our student enrichment program. Also in getting counsellors to go this distance for work would be a problem."[16]

Boyle saw another difficulty. "Another problem," he said, "would be the public school system in Sheridan. Whether they would be open to our program or not."[17]

The cost of Sheridan was not out of line, for the Jesuits were willing to take "a considerable loss." The estimated cost of new buildings on the present site was one and one-half million "with costs going up every month." The Sheridan property could be acquired "probably for one million," but many costly adjustments, like the construction of a gymnasium, would have to be paid. In the end, Boyle brushed off the proposal with a brief remark, "Any further interest in this area should be pursued by the Trustees of the Home." Since the Trustees showed no "further interest" the matter was dropped.

This report, which had been composed by Hamilton, Boyle's assistant at this time, reveals two current improvements, reflecting Dr. Marsh's growing influence: Staff members were attending professional studies part time in Portland's institutions of higher learning. Secondly, specialized classes, including "student enrichment programs" were getting more attention. The Beaverton School District was gradually being drawn in, at first as supplementary staff members, and eventually as administrators and instructors, by contract, for the entire school program.

Subsequent budgets for the Home reflected these changes. On January 24, 1970, Father Park provided the trustees with the sobering data on escalating costs:

1966 .... $120,415
1967 147,964
1968 160,651
1969 236,798
[Estimated] 1970 .... 256,446[18]

One must keep in mind that these figures represent costs for fewer boys, approximately forty for the 1970 calendar year. Also, these were operating costs only. The state and county had raised their contributions significantly, but as the Home's share of cost increased, other risks of deficits mounted proportionately. Sooner or later there would be an unpleasant show down.

Demolition of Main

As often happens, staff members were not fully aware of the advice of experts regarding some of the problem areas on the campus. In 1970, the maintenance of Main was simply not possible. Several independent studies had been made, all of them reaching the same conclusion. The building could not be saved without expenditures far exceeding practicality. Boyle's report to both boards, the trustees and the advisors, was carefully reviewed and supported. Thus it happened, that despite the very vocal opposition of many, the order was given for the inevitable. Main had to go.

While Boyle was designing new uses for other buildings, to replace the loss of Main, another complication arose. Boyle wrote about it to Sister Angela in Santa Cruz.

> *Our building program is being held up for three to five years due to the moratorium on sewer annexations as set up September 5th, 1969 so that we cannot lease any of our land until the moratorium is lifted. The bank was to have financed the new construction.*[19]

So much for the building program. Boyle saw no reason why the demolition of Main should be put off. He presented plans at the annual meeting of the trustees.

> *Father Boyle reported on demolition plans for the main building. There were three bids for the job, and Colhouer Construction Co. presented the lowest bid of $9,000. The manager of the company agreed verbally to reduce the bid by $1,000 before the bids were opened, so the company's final bid was $8,000. The second bid was for $14,000 and the third bid for $18,000. Demolition by Colhouer Co. will take place between July 20 and July 30. The plan is for the debris to be placed in the swamp behind the barn. The trustees suggested relocating the dump area for debris across the creek on property reserved for the future Home development, to avoid a problem in the future sale or lease of the property that is marked for commercial development.*[20]

On July 30, a bulldozer leveled old Main "in a cloud of dust." The Marian statue nearby remained unharmed and Boyle announced afterwards that it would "be moved to a similar place of honor when a new school is built." He added that "it would be at least two years before there is a new school building and it would be at a new location facing S.W. 170th."[21]

Introducing Father William Hamilton

In the criticism which followed the demise of the venerable structure, Boyle had to bear the brunt of the blame. He was already being blamed because the projected building blitz had fizzled out. There seems to have been more reasons than the moratorium for this, but no one was talking about them. Whatever the case, the cooling off period following the initial euphoria was a painful time for Boyle, who found it necessary for health reasons, to take time off from his directorship. Father Park served in his place for the few weeks of his absence.

He was assisted by Father William Hamilton, who eagerly studied the subtleties of the Behavior Modification Program under the tutelage of Dr. Marsh. Hamilton had been interested in child care since his seminary days, when he spent his summer months at St. Mary's. He had become so attached to the Home that he requested to be assigned there after ordination.

He looked like a model for the part. A large crop of dark hair, with a husky nape on the back of his head, similar to illustrations of Mark Twain, and heavy sideburns, gave him the appearance of a benevolent young executive who understood the foibles of growing boys. While his bearing expressed a no-nonsense philosophy, his countenance, framed by the popular hair style, demonstrated that he was a member of the "now generation." In winning the confidence of the boys, this was a no mean asset.

Rev. Wm. Hamilton reminiscing with boys.

Hamilton, like Goodrich, had an uncommon talent for public relations. He was better than Goodrich when it came to composing letters or articles for coaxing money from hard-nosed bureaucrats. With his talent he could have run a four ring circus. He had the energy, the know how, and the motivation. It was sometimes said, out of earshot of course, that he was after Boyle's job. If so, he got it sooner than he expected, because Boyle, a short time after his return to Beaverton, submitted his resignation to the Archbishop.

Departure of Father Boyle

To explain his decision, Boyle stated publicly that he had completed what he was asked to do. The Home was on a firm financial basis. Decisions regarding its priorities and campus development had been made. Its reputation as a professional institution had been improved. With the blessing of his Excellency, he left Beaverton for The Dalles, Oregon, where he put his talent to work.

Hamilton's title when he succeeded Boyle, was "acting director." On March 5, 1971, Archbishop Dwyer informed the trustees that Hamilton had been confirmed in his position. He was now called "Executive Director."

Hamilton was present at this meeting. He reported that "the 1971 operating budget includes adequate income for the Home, because of new programs providing tax funds at a level nearer the cost of the program." Father Park, the board's secretary, recorded an additional tidbit, which suggests that the quest for a new campus was still active.

> *Regarding a building program, Father Hamilton also reported the Franciscan Sisters' retreat house has a price of $800,000 which with necessary additions would cost the Boys Home over 1 million dollars. The plans drawn by Norman and Stanich would cost about one and one-quarter million dollars. If the retreat house price were low enough, the Boys Home would be interested in it.*[22]

Since the meeting adjourned after this last report, there is no documented evidence of a decision regarding the acquisition of the retreat house. In the minutes of the following trustee meeting on May 5, 1971, this proposal does not appear. The trustees authorized Hamilton to give the gym two coats of paint, to purchase two vans and to provide "some blacktopping in the area of the old Main building."

To pay for these improvements, he was directed to hold a public auction for the sale of the farm machinery, which was no longer in use. Five thousand dollars, it was said, would be realized from the auction. Later the auction was conducted by a local auctioneer, to the immense delight of the boys and the neighbors. The barn had gone up in flames, the machinery was distributed like hot dogs at a baseball game, in the presence of a crowd and with lots of noise, and all that was left was a tractor.

Retreat House Property

The legal status of the retreat house was still in limbo. The Sisters' offer to sell, no doubt, was prompted by the defective title to the property. The complex contained forty rooms, kitchen, dining rooms, chapel and other desirable facilities, which could serve well as a boys home. It occupied twenty-five acres of the original fifty received from the Archdiocese, contingent upon the Sisters' continuance at the Home. When this contract of gift land was drawn up, neither party could foresee the unfavorable happenings in the Sisters' future. Doubts now regarding the Sisters' present intention of remaining at the Home, because of circumstances largely beyond their control, raised questions concerning the legal and moral problems for both parties.

By 1970, the Sisters' had honored their contract for seventeen years. They had developed the retreat house and they had paid taxes faithfully on the unused half of the property. They wanted to sell this undeveloped half.

Mr. R.A. McQuarry was business manager for the Archdiocese. When the Sisters requested leave to sell this, he reminded them of their contingent ownership and suggested a compromise which recognized the services of the Sisters for the seventeen years. The Archdiocese, he wrote, would cancel the conditions on ownership of the property where the retreat house stood. In the sale of the balance, both parties to the original contract would share the returns.[23] The Sisters agreed. A new contract, replacing the first, was approved by the chancery in Portland and the council in Santa Cruz. The Sisters' undisputed title to the retreat house left them free to work out their problems at the Home.

There was no simple answer to these problems. Only two Sisters remained at the Home. Sister Carmela and Sister Dolores were the last remnant of as many as eighteen at one time. Most of the missing sixteen had left the community, in part because of the community's failure to give more support to the social apostolate, a high priority in their generation. Several of these sisters remained at St. Mary's as lay staff. They were: Sister Patrick Maureen (Mary Ellen Cox); Sister John Francis (Mary Kay Correia Garcia); Sister Josepha (Yvonne LeClerc Rogers); Sister Basil Margeruite (Ellen Tone Olson); and Sister M. Peter (Emma Grosz-Dennis).

They all made a significant contribution to the Home, the new treatment program, and the boys. They were extremely dedicated, loyal, and totally unselfish in giving of themselves. Two, who dedicated the majority of their adult lives to St. Mary's, have since died of cancer.

Mary Ellen Cox died March, 1987, and Mary Kay Correia Garcia died October, 1988, after 24 years and 17 years of dedicated service.

Before the arrival of Hamilton, Boyle had tried to persuade Sister Angela to send more Sisters. He wrote that the future of the Home "was very bleak as far as the Sisters were concerned." Then he added, "I look around the city of Portland alone and see abandoned Convent buildings and much to my foresight, hopefully, I'll not see such a sight here at St. Mary's . . . . The whole idea of religious influence in the child's school life is now almost lost within the structure of a lay body of school personnel."[24]

Dolores and Carmela lived in makeshift quarters. In 1970, from January to December, their combined income was $9,581.22. Their costs of living, including rent, were $10,094.29, leaving a deficit of $513.07. They were not big spenders. Their total cost of clothing, for example for two years, 1970 – 1971, was $383.31. Total cost for car and travel for the same two years was almost the same, $381.34.[25]

The Group Home

The Motherhouse, in view of its losses, did not see how to improve its relations with the Home. Dolores and Carmela were like two pioneers on the frontier, loyal to the home base but reluctant to leave their posts. They kept in touch by contributing monthly trivia about the boys and themselves to the Sisters' *Newsletter* published in Santa Cruz.

Dolores usually composed the copy for the *Newsletter.* The following item, which she sent, alludes to the group home.

> *On February 28th [1972], there will be some guests to begin discussions about a foster home program in which prospective foster home parents will be taught the ideas of behavior modification, the system under which we work. A study has been made of our former students; 75% made it and*

> *the failure of the 25% seems to come mainly from the homes in which they were sent, going from one type of care to a home in which there is no further contact with our methods and psychology of help. Also, there are plans to open another group home.*[26]

Reference to this group home requires additional comment. A chronic problem at St. Mary's involved post-treatment care. More often than not, boys who had been successfully treated and released at St. Mary's, had no place to go. The homes from which they had come usually were responsible for their being at a treatment center in the first place. Marsh had proposed group homes as the solution, residences with group parents, or supervision depending upon need, where boys could mature and adapt to normal society. Hamilton agreed. In his St. Mary's Home for Boys Report for July 28, 1972, he included the following.

> *We opened an off-campus home in Forest Grove this past October, as an Achievement House. This was started as a pilot project, over a 10 month period, to see if this would increase the learning skills, of our boys who were ready to leave the institutional setting, but not ready to return home. Our success rate was phenomenal. Seven boys were advanced to the Achievement House and while there, there was no incidence of running away, no encounters with the law, no major acting out behavior exhibited and every boy progressed in school and in the home environment.*
>
> *Unfortunately, the Achievement House program has been suspended for 60 days due to our financial difficulties. We anticipate, however, that the State will increase our funding by October.*[27]

Actually, the group home did not open again for several years. Recalling the incident, one staff member noted that Hamilton threatened to close the group home if the state would not provide more money. "And the state called his bluff, so he had to close it."

This appears to be the case, as it is confirmed by what Glennis McNeel wrote for the *Valley Times*.

> *A group home in Forest Grove for teenage boys with emotional problems, "a successful home — we never had one runaway or brush with the law, and the boys were doing well in public school" faces closure because of inadequate financing from the State of Oregon, according to Father William*

> Hamilton, director of St. Mary's Home for Boys, Aloha, St. Mary's operates the group home.
> Fr. Hamilton stated that the $25 cost per day per child in the Forest Grove facility is being reimbursed by the state at $16, part of current fiscal procedures that are causing the Home to run a $6,500 monthly deficit.
> Purchase of care amounts tendered to the Boy's Home are the lowest in the State, Fr. Hamilton said. Although jobs that used to be filled by members of religious orders are now staffed by salaried lay people, the State-ordered price freeze will continue to July 1973, he said.
> If no substantial increase is granted the Home in 1973, Father Hamilton said the entire operation will close and the 51 resident boys returned to Dammasch, detention homes, State Hospital or to the home communities where they have already failed.[28]

Hamilton had other choice comments about the State's freeze program while bureaucrats investigated costs. He concluded this interview with some not-so-subtle threats.

> Another source of dismay to the program director is his feeling that decision makers don't know what is going on.
> "When has the State ever come out to see our program? Not the people who make decisions on funding. Legislators aren't aware, either. In the time I've been Director, no legislator has come by to say, 'We're spending a lot of money here. What's going on?' Elected officials should be responsible for being aware of what's going on in their own area," he said.
> Unless additional financial help from State or private sources is provided to St. Mary's, it appears the seven teens now living successfully in the Forest Grove community may be the first to find themselves thrown back on the resources of the community.

Similar interviews appeared elsewhere. One gets the impression, seeing them gathered together, that Hamilton was enjoying the alleged crisis. When it was all over, he had lost the group home, but he had gained in the long run. On April 23, 1974, he reported to the members of the Advisory Board. "We have received," he said, "a commitment from the State of Oregon for a higher level of financing for St. Mary's Home itself as opposed to the group home."

One suspects that State officials were delighted to be rid of Hamilton for awhile. It was very difficult to defend themselves against all of the noise he was making and they could not attack him because his engaging smiles and emotional appeals for the boys had captivated the public.

Every Boy Is Treatable

In the *Newsletter,* Dolores had more to offer. This concerned the relationship between Dr. Marsh and members of the staff. Marsh, admittedly, tended to place "continuing pressures" on staff members "for excellence" in their professional service. Sometime later he worried about their reaction to this. Had they disliked him because of it?

Success in their profession, he had often reminded them, depended upon them and not upon the boys. At times he sounded like Father Flanagan at Boys Town near Omaha, where he lived before coming to Portland. "If any boy admitted to St. Mary's fails, it is not his fault. It is ours. Every boy is treatable. We may not have the tools yet, but every boy is treatable."

Doubtlessly, Marsh will be pleased to read what Dolores wrote about this in the *Newsletter.*

> The staff have been having sessions with Dr. Marsh on Thursday afternoons and he believes that if we have to send out a boy without having helped him, somehow it is the fault of the staff. So . . . sometimes it isn't the Boy's attitude that needs to be changed but the staff's attitude. Once you really realize what we are doing, the defensive attitude can go and we really become more equipped to help the boy. It is thrilling to me, and I think I have changed a whole lot in my ability to respond positively and to find ways to help and interest the boy. We still have a big task before us, but I am thoroughly enjoying it.[29]

The Departure of the Franciscan Missionary Sisters

The enthusiasm of Dolores and the dedication of Carmela, greatly impressed the "Executive Director" who soon became anxious about their health. Unwittingly he triggered the final decision of the motherhouse by expressing his anxieties in a letter to the Superior General.

> As you know St. Mary's has undergone some radical changes in it's treatment modality to service emotionally disturbed children. The boys are hard core behavior management problem children who exhibit a great deal of anti-social and bizarre behavior. It demands a great deal of on-going training and stamina to deal with this type of behavioral exhibition, and I feel Sister Dolores is running out of stamina. I fear that her health, both physical and mental will not be able to keep up with this program direction.[30]

Then Hamilton added a gallant tribute to both Sisters.

> Sister Dolores has contributed greatly to the development of the many boys who have passed through the program at St. Mary's Boys Home. For this reason she cannot be praised enough; your Order can be proud of her.
> Sister Carmela is doing an outstanding job in her position.

At a cabinet meeting eleven days later, on March 2, 1974, Hamilton's letter received more than ordinary attention. As reported in the minutes of the meeting, this is what happened.

> Sister Angela read a letter from Fr. Hamilton of St. Mary's Home in Beaverton . . . . We discussed the possibility of withdrawing from the Boys Home in Beaverton as soon as possible.
> Motion: I move that we write a letter to Fr. Hamilton advising him that we are considering his request in the letter of February 21 and that we will give him a decision as soon as possible.
> Motion: I move that Sister Raymond be delegated to see Archbishop Dwyer in person to present Fr. Hamilton's letter and to ask how we can withdraw from the Boys Home as the council feels that the Home has undergone such radical changes that it is not what the Franciscan Missionary Sisters of Our Lady of Sorrows originally agreed to staff in 1953.[31]

At the following Cabinet meeting in Santa Cruz on March 16, 1974, another motion was made, seconded and passed as follows:

> I move that Sister Dolores and Sister Carmela be reassigned to other missions in June after the school year of 1974 and that no other Sisters be assigned to replace them at St. Mary's Home for Boys.[32]

Sister M. Carmela *Sister M. Delores*

The *Newsletter* for May 1974 carried the faintly upbeat declaration by Dolores, who was already on the far side of exhaustion. "Sister Carmela and I," she wrote, "will be leaving the Boys Home. Sister's last day will be the end of May . . . . School doesn't end until June 7th. There are many, many memories but this is just the right time for the change. Doors close and new doors open."

When the last of the Franciscan Missionary Sisters departed from St. Mary's, they bore many gifts. They left behind, however, a dear and trusted friend, their former colleague in the community. Emma Dennis, formerly Sister M. Peter, would succeed Father Hamilton as the first lay director of St. Mary's. She was currently the director's indispensable assistant, the efficient organizer behind the throne.

Chapter 9

The Recent Years

WHEN THE FRANCISCAN Sisters left the Boys Home in June, there was a new Archbishop in Portland. Archbishop Dwyer, emotionally devastated by what he believed was happening to the American Church, and physically weakened by cancer of the pancreas, resigned his see in early 1974 and left Portland for Piedmont, California, a suburb of Oakland. He died there less than two years later.[1]

Cornelius Power, heretofore second Bishop of Yakima, was installed as the seventh Archbishop of Portland in Oregon on April 17, 1974. Warm hearted and readily approachable, the new prelate was as unlike his predecessor as salt and pepper. He had been a popular bishop in Yakima, so hopes were high at the Home that he would support its badly needed rebuilding program.

Father Hamilton, waited for an opportune time to get his attention. With reason he was more than merely anxious about the turnover in his Board of Advisors and staff, the one because its members felt left out in the making of decisions, and the other because its members felt underpaid. They said that their salary scale was lower than the scale in similar institutions. Both groups had been agitating for change in a polite manner, while Hamilton scrambled for funds and pleaded with the Chancery for means to appease them.

Meanwhile, there were more mundane problems. The most irritating of these, apparently, was the lack of space occasioned by the loss of Main and the proliferation of staff members and programs. Students from local colleges were conducting on-going research projects under Marsh. They, too, required space somewhere for interviews and examination of records. A temporary solution, it was decided, was the rental of mobile units. Business Manager, Bob Tobiassen, at a Board of Advisors meeting on August 28, 1974, stated that St. Mary's had contracted for two trailers, each with two classrooms, for the cost of $700 per month. The agreement, Bob explained, had been made for a two year period only, by which time it was hoped current expectations for a new campus would be realized.

Eleven years later, the trailers were still there and two more were added, one of them to serve as additional office space. Soon all of them were permanent fixtures, scarcely noticed when one's eyes swept across the campus. There they were, surrounded by flowers and shrubs, no longer reminders of what might have been.

The Archbishop, of course, had been informed of the innovations. Perhaps he had got the hint. After all, renting trailers for classrooms could mean only one thing. Hamilton decided it was time to press for two concessions: changes on the controlling board and partial control of the land decisions.

> *It is time, [he wrote], to move ahead with community involvement now to the extent that our community leaders be a part of the governing body of St. Mary's Inc.*
>
> *Our Advisory Board had requested this under Archbishop Dwyer who responded favorably but postponed a decision because of his resignation. Our statement of request is that we meet very soon to present our recommendations for A) Board Consolidation and B) Legal definition of Land Ownership.*[2]

In his conclusion, Hamilton presented supplementary information to influence his cause.

"St. Mary's," he said, "was in its 83rd year of continued service to disadvantaged boys serving an average of 71 boys per year." To date, it had cared for 5,900 boys.

The Archbishop was sympathetic. It was commonly known that he did not rush into hasty decisions. He informed the director that he would appoint committees to study both suggestions.

Others in the Chancery were more pragmatic. They could foresee long delays in the development of the Beaverton land. The St.

Mary's campus, they urged, should remain fundamentally as it was for the time being. Major repairs and alterations should be made to comply with the fire marshal's directives, but a final decision in rebuilding the campus should be postponed until the committees' reports were in.

They also said that efforts to find an alternative site on cheaper land should be continued.

The Year Ad Dominum 1977

Some years are better than others. Some are worse. During some, giant strides are made, and during others, no progress at all is visible.

The year 1977 was one like the latter. It was not a year of earth shaking accomplishments, but one of bringing countless little problems into focus and resolving them, no matter how tedious or boring. In this period of transition, it marked a new level of professional maturity as a treatment center. In part this process had been forced by legal requirements connected with substantial state support. If some of the requirements appeared to be picky, they were important for the record. "St. Mary's," Dr. Marsh noted dryly, "had become more sophisticated," meaning also more subtle and more highly structured. Suddenly questions like this were discussed endlessly in the board meetings.

Under what circumstances could the per diem be collected for a runaway boy who returns seven days later?

Or:

To what extent is St. Mary's liable for damage done by a boy while visiting a guest home?

Sometimes the problem was not so much willingness to keep contractual agreements as understanding what they meant. Gone were the good old days when sorting the boys' socks was a major operation.

Big Money

The new order of things also meant new records in budgets.

In his proposed budget for the year 1977-1978, Hamilton reported to Archbishop Power that St. Mary's anticipated an income from their two major sources, the State of Oregon and United Way, of $780,000. This, he added, was only 75% of the cost. In the following years, the projected cost for an average of 43 boys in residence "would be about $55 per day" for each boy, or something in excess of $810,000. Hamilton presented other particulars.

> This past year, we have been extensively involved in building renovation. We have invested $105,000 to cover most of our buildings, in order to comply with the Health and Fire Department codes. All of this money we received through grants or emergency funds from the state . . . . I anticipate that to be in full compliance, we need to renovate Christie Cottage at an expense of about $65,000.[3]

In early April, Hamilton wrote to the chairman of his Advisory Board, Robert Oringdulph, that the Archbishop had appointed a new Trustee Board. "I do know they were selected with the primary instruction to deal with the land problem." Later in the same month, staff member Bob Tobiassen, informed the Administrative Council, a kind of cabinet recently established by Hamilton, that salaries and benefits for staff members had been worked out. Salaries, according to Hamilton, had been in compliance with law for sometime, salaries were comparable with those in similar institutions.

Dr. Marsh, meanwhile, watched the improvement of campus facilities with considerable relief, but also with a certain wariness about its influence on overall results. He was concerned mostly about the priority of the spirit and the need for research. In September 1977, he brought his reflections to the attention of the Senior staff.

> Dr. Marsh stated that in the past additional monies and staff were seen as a panacea to any difficulties St. Mary's was encountering. Obviously, this has not been the answer as our chronic problems still exist. Additionally, it is felt that staff depends a lot on materialistic reinforcers in the treatment program, when the most valuable reinforcers are social. Therefore, the senior staff are asked to make more constructive use of staff and when asking for additional staff to consider thoroughly the use of the staff, training and the benefits that staff will be able to provide the entire program. Conversely, staff should consider how best to use existing funds that are available.[4]

The staff was impressed, but the topic on most minds was still the land, which by this time was generally believed to be worth millions of dollars. What Marsh said was doubtlessly true, but who could ignore the significance of what was taking place around them, an unprecedented land boom in their very own backyard.

More About Land

The Beaverton land, including the approximately twenty-eight acres on which St. Mary's was built, still belong legally to the Archdiocese. Its use by law could be determined by the Archbishop and the Board of Trustees he appointed. This board, additionally, had a moral obligation to use the land to benefit the Catholic Church for which most of it had been purchased with church money. The balance, the so-called Levi Anderson land, had apparently been purchased with a legacy, which required certain obligations. These, according to competent legal authority, had been honored. There remains the question of generosity on the part of the Archdiocese.

In the *Catholic Sentinel* for July 22, 1977, Father Park refers to the Archdiocese's support of St. Mary's.

"The question is often asked, he said, "could the funding used at St. Mary's be better used somewhere else in the Church?" He answers his own question by saying "No" to Catholic readers, because, as he states, "Most of the monies used at St. Mary are from the government and cannot be used for specific religious purposes."

The question was a legitimate one. Catholics at this time were hard pressed to maintain their school system, which was disintegrating at an alarming rate. In recent years never more than five percent of St. Mary's residents were Catholic. How then, could Catholics neglect their own priorities, their schools, to endow the Boys Home? This is what many Catholics were saying and the Archbishop could not ignore them.

"We receive no financial assistance [directly] from the Archdiocese," Father Hamilton stated in the same article quoted above, "although the Archdiocese lets us use land and buildings rent free. We are extremely pleased that the Church continues to sponsor care for children by providing buildings and land and lending us its name to give us legitimacy . . . ."

This is the dilemma of the Archdiocese. Board members at the Home tended to think that the Archdiocese, in a spirit of fidelity to its long mission at the Home, if not to honor the legacy of Levi

Anderson, should deed the twenty-eight acres to the Home. The last word on this touchy subject has yet to be said.

A Meeting of Both Boards

In December 1977, both boards gathered at St. Mary's to discuss an "overview" and the delicate subject of the land. Archbishop Power presided. Hamilton and Marsh took turns in responding to questions raised by the Trustees.

The Archbishop wanted to know more about the "delinquent" status of the boys and about the school program.

"Delinquency," Hamilton answered, "has increased tremendously in the last five years due to family breakdown and the lack of discipline in the schools." He termed this a "collapse of the system" because both the family and school had stopped making certain demands and allowed anti-social behavior. He also pointed out that the legal apparatus of the country encouraged this by making it more difficult to discipline and control juveniles. Instead of accepting discipline, children could withdraw through pot, alcohol and other stimulants, and through watching television.

Dr. Marsh noted that St. Mary's had established an excellent record in reversing delinquency for some. "There is an approximate success rate of 70% and is based on the boys return to the family . . ." Parents were now being brought into the treatment program to learn how to manage their boy's behavior. "Judges often tell offending boys either to make it at St. Mary's or end up at MacLaren."

MacLaren, of course, was the end of the line.

There were other questions and a recess. Then came the million dollar subject. Mr. Oringdulph, Chairman of the Advisory Board, asked the Archbishop about land development. It was the moment for which they had all waited. What followed is reported in the Minutes.

> *Mr. Oringdulph next brought up the matter of property development and the Trustee Board meeting of November 3rd, 1977. Archbishop Power then explained that the Trustees were addressing the problem of selling the land for the "highest amount and best use" and consequently he wished to hear from the Advisory Board as to goals and financial requirements of*

the Home. He suggested that the Advisory Board consider the operation of the school as if there were no land in question but that the school would be looking to the Archdiocese for support. The Archbishop suggested that the Advisory Board submit plans for enlarging or bettering the school and let the Archdiocese decide how to fund.[5]

This is not what the Advisors wanted to hear. Doubtlessly aware of their disappointment, the Archbishop then stated "that the Trustees wish meaningful communication with the Advisory Board and that there should be no problem in this regard."

The year 1977 ended as it had begun. "It was a year of preoccupation," Emma Dennis said, "with the termination of policies and procedures that had ruled in the past." From this time on it would be an entirely different ball game with few familiar sounds. Only some of the landmarks were left, and a certain nostalgia in the minds of some of the older alumni.

St. Mary's Alumni

By this time, evidence of alumni success began to be noticed. There had been, as noted above, war heroes and priests. Proportionate to its size, St. Mary's had many of both.

An Alumni Association had been formed many years earlier, in 1927, when the Home was called St. Mary's High School and the neighboring town Huber. Father Joseph Heesacker was superintendent and Jim Robinson was "the Professor" to the Sisters. A spirit of pious respectability pervaded the place then, like benediction incense in the kitchen. In the following year, as evidence of the school's orthodoxy, the first year book was published. It was called *La Maria*. A special place was reserved in it for an account about the new Alumni Association.

> *St. Mary's Alumni association consists of former students of St. Mary's high school, and in addition to that all those in various walks of life who were at one time inmates of St. Mary's Home for Boys. It was organized last year and after a spirited election Eugene Schulte, '26, was elected president. Gene is attending Columbia University, Portland . . . .*

> *The secretary's voluminous correspondence has disclosed the fact that several former St. Mary's boys have risen high in this world's affairs. Perhaps our most loyal Alumnus is Joseph Geroux of The Dalles, who bears the distinction of being the first boy to pass the portals of St. Mary's Home back in '89. Joseph is now a prosperous merchant of The Dalles, and every year in addition to furnishing us all the garden seeds we need, sends a gold medal for general excellence to the boy having the best scholastic record.*
>
> *Another to win fame and renown is Lawrence Farnsworth, who holds the enviable position of foreign dramatic critic for the New York American, and New York Journal. Lawrence is also a poet and dramatist of no mean ability. Some of his tragedies have been produced on the stage in London while his poems in both French and English have been published in many parts of our country and Europe.*
>
> *Among students of the latter day we find Frank Spiering, a salesman for the Metropolitan Life Insurance Co., the Cellini brothers operating a dairy ranch at Galt, Calif., while the U.S. service carries on its roll such names as George Flett, Fritz Marquart, John Rutkowski, Alex Keegan, Lawrence O'Neill and Theodore Vaughn.*

Not all war heroes had died. Ricardo Martinez, whose appearance suggested that of a prosperous cattle rancher somewhere in New Mexico, lived at St. Mary's from 1934, when he was only six years old, until 1946. After a distinguished career in the military, he turned to research on the bottomless subject of the American Indian. Having come from an Indian-Mexican background, he took naturally to his studies, accumulating in time, a near definitive bibliography for the use of other scholars.[6]

Another Indian graduate is Edison Chiloquin, whose portrait occupies a prominent place in Heesacker Hall. Edison's appearance reminds one of the image on the back of some nickels, which are probably collector's items. He belongs to the Klamath tribe. When the Klamath's reservation land was "terminated," as they described it two decades ago, Edison protested it in the only way he knew how: he refused to use the money he received for his share of the sale. "Edison Chiloquin wanted his land," an anonymous observer wrote some years ago. "So he lit a sacred fire. He kept this fire burning for over five years. By that time the government gave the land back."

The First Reunion

Both Edison and Ricardo have left lasting impressions, but not many other Indians have. "We had many Indians here," said Adam Heineman, meaning "over the years."

One should not be surprised at this, since the area where the Home now stands was once occupied by the Tuality tribe, whose ghosts have dwelled ever since in the woods around the tule ponds. Otherwise all evidence of the Tuality has disappeared, like Adam's "many Indians" at St. Mary's.

Some alumni, the palefaces in particular, are never committed to anything identified with their past. Happily rootless, or possibly shy, they prefer to remain "out there" in the mists of oblivion. Others rise to the surface and seek their former companions by holding what we call "reunions." These reunions are fashionable today and they are excellent opportunities to show one's fine figure, or stylish clothes. Some who attend them, however, have loftier motives.

Two of these were Dick Hansen and Adam Heineman, who have been mentioned before. It was Dick Hansen, in his home in Auburn, California, who first suggested to Adam that they should organize a St. Mary's reunion. It was Adam who grabbed the suggestion like a trout taking a fly. With the help of the Sisters of St. Mary's, especially Sister Christina, and former Superintendents Father Gerace and Father Goodrich, Adam assembled names and addresses and issued invitations for the first formal reunion on June 19, 1978.

It was celebrated at St. Mary's of the Valley High School and

Alumni gather to reminisce. (l to r) Frank Sullivan, Dick Hansen, Edison Chiloquin and Adam Heineman.

everyone there proclaimed it "a huge success." Sixty-five of the "boys," as the Sisters preferred to call them, showed up for fried chicken and a chance to inspect their former colleagues. Twenty of the Sisters of St. Mary were there to welcome them. Also, "about ten priests," including some of the former superintendents. Nothing could have kept Gerace, Maxwell, or Goodrich away.

But the celebrity of the day was Archbishop Howard. This venerable old prelate was in his one hundred and first year, but he made it to the celebration, two hundred yards distant, on his own steam.[7] He was in retirement in a small residence on the grounds of the Sisters of St. Mary Motherhouse. "He intended to stay [at the reunion] five minutes," Adam said, "but he stayed two hours and made a stirring presentation. He turned the reunion into an event of honoring the priests and nuns who took care of us."

The party did not break up that first reunion night until nine o'clock, a time that the Sisters, if not all of the "boys", should have been home in bed.[8]

Flipping hamburgers to feed the alumni.

Renewed Efforts to Relocate

The next five years of St. Mary's history were dominated by land values and the campus rebuilding and/or relocation. While Dr. Marsh and his professional staff continued to search for better methods of treatment and higher percentages of success, the director and his board members were occupied almost totally in searching for answers to their long standing problems of land and the physical plant.

The Home still occupied 28 acres in 1982. These had an estimated worth of $55,000 per acre, totalling in value $1,540,000. Was it appropriate, board members asked themselves, to remain on land of this value, while their antiquated buildings worth 15% of this amount, continued to disintegrate? They did not think so.

Their efforts for finding another site proceeded with almost desperate urgency. Brief clips from the Minutes of the Advisory Board reveal some of the particulars of the process.[9]

> *September 11, 1980. Property Issue* was discussed and it was explained that the land is owned by the Archdiocese of Portland and St. Mary's Boys Home. The "Five Year Plan" ties into a possible sale, in that we have a plan for the future.
>
> *December 11, 1980. The Five Year Plan* was introduced by Father Hamilton. [There followed two motions urging the approval of a Vocational Group Home made possible by the land development.]
>
> *June 11, 1981. St. Mary's Boys Home Land Sale* was discussed and it was explained to the Advisory Board that certain parcels of property have been sold to Tektronix and Floating Points. The revenue will go to the Archdiocese in a trust fund. The revenue (interest) from the fund will be used for different programs in the Archdiocese including St. Mary's Boys Home. The Home will have to apply for the grant. It was suggested that St. Mary's should be looking for a new site and Father Hamilton was escorted to a parcel of property within Washington County that is for sale for approximately $5,000 per acre. This parcel contained 80 acres. It was moved that the Facilities Committee, chaired by Mimi Morissette, be directed to make a study and start investigating the possibility of acquiring a new site for St. Mary's Boys Home and that this committee report back to the total Advisory Board at the time of the next meeting.
>
> *September 17, 1981.* The first item to be discussed on the agenda was the **Land Purchase.** Fr. Hamilton displayed a map of the particular parcel to be used as a future site . . . . Father then distributed copies of a proposal to the Board of Trustees.
>
> *March 11, 1982.* Thru (sic) Bob McQuarry, Father Hamilton learned that the Archbishop wants us to use our

> *reserves to purchase a future land site. For this reason Father feels that a Position Paper must be developed, which would include St. Mary's philosophy, goals, future plans, etc. The direction of this paper would be based on our desire to move. St Mary's currently sits on 28 acres valued at approximately $55,000 per acre. The site we are interested in, near Rock Creek, consists of 80 acres valued at approximately $5,000 per acre.*
>
> ***May 20, 1982. Why St. Mary's Needs to Relocate*** *[there followed eighty minutes discussion on means for resolving the problems of Trustees' approval and financing.]*

By this time, the Archdiocese had begun the actual sale of the Beaverton property. The first public announcement regarding this appeared in the *Catholic Sentinel* on April 10, 1981. This report contained the following: "Archbishop Power has established a perpetual endowment for the Archdiocese to be funded initially through the entire net cash proceeds from the sale of 520 acres surrounding St. Mary's Home for Boys, Beaverton." Three weeks later, an extensive article in the *Catholic Sentinel* provided a detailed history of the acquisition of the land and its disposition, with an important map to clarify certain obscurities.[10]

In the course of all of the happy excitement, occasioned by these revelations, the Archbishop made it clear that St. Mary's had not been forgotten and that it would share in the benefits of the new endowment.

The New Transition Program

The Archbishop's encouragement was not wasted. St. Mary's staff soon plunged into another creative experimental program, which Marsh had advocated all along. A Group Home had been tried earlier, without surviving, allegedly, because Hamilton's bluff was called by someone tougher than he was. This was not the end of the road, however, and at the Board of Advisors meeting on October 6, 1982, Hamilton introduced the new plan. It was reported in the Minutes as follows.

> ***S.M.I.L.E. Program*** *(St. Mary's Independent Living Environment) Gary Ford was introduced by Fr. Hamilton. An off-campus group home was initially part of St. Mary's Five Year Plan, and Gary has spent a year designing this new pro-*

gram. The Meyer Foundation submitted start-up funds of $12,500 and Dr. Marsh donated the duplex housing for the program. Gary is the Program Coordinator. S.M.I.L.E. opened in August with 4 boys living on their own (St. Mary's provides the back-up facility.)[11]

This program evolved into two: the "Transition Home," the second step following treatment on the St. Mary's campus, with resident supervision by the Home's staff; and, the "Independent Living Program," the third and last step "which simulates an independent living situation as closely as possible under a less supervised environment . . . . In the latter each boy is responsible for his share of living expenses in the apartment, including rent, utilities, telephone, garbage, transportation and entertainment. He will contribute a certain percentage in accordance to his monthly earnings. Upon graduation this money will be returned to him."[12]

Both apartments used in these off-campus programs had been donated by Dr. Marsh.

Treatment Program

One other major innovation appeared during Hamilton's tenure as Executive Director. In a recent book published by St. Mary's and co-authored by Dr. Marsh, Patrick Connell and Ellen Olson, Marsh provides an "Historical Overview," in which he writes:

> *It had been observed from the beginning of the treatment program that boys referred to St. Mary's were often the victims of sexual abuse, and sometimes abusers themselves. Until quite recently, it was infrequent that a boy was referred specifically because of his sexual offenses. Usually this information was only incidental if contained within the case history. It was most often discovered while the boy was on campus. Sexual acting out had been treated mainly with negative consequences and/or ignoring the behavior.*
>
> *As the numbers of identified sexually disturbed adolescents began to increase, the problem received more attention. Staff were trained to be sex therapists and to assess sexual problems. In 1983, St. Mary's launched the initial phase of its Sexual Treatment Program. The service of Dr. Kevin McGovern were initially secured. He provided the staff with concepts of sexual*

treatment and current theory regarding the sexually disturbed, both the victim as well as the offender. Following Dr. McGovern's input, various members of the professional staff attended seminars and training programs directed specifically toward sexual disorder and current treatments.[13]

"We have borrowed heavily from the experience of others with adults and children," Marsh continued, "and have developed our own systems, dealing with adolescents."

Nationwide attention has been focused on this unique St. Mary's program. Boys from nine different states have been placed at the Home for treatment, which is generally regarded as the best of its kind.

When Dr. Marsh arrived at St. Mary's, it was threatened with almost immediate bankruptcy. Today it is flourishing, with a longer list of applicants than it can accommodate in many years to come.

The Hamilton Years in Retrospect

As director, Father Hamilton lasted four more years. Thus his tenure in office was one of the longest in the history of St. Mary's, sixteen years. In retrospect, he has been regarded as the most controversial administrator in the long history of St. Mary's. He was responsible for many changes, not all of them acceptable to priests of the Archdiocese, who complained openly about his methods of raising money and even more significantly about his decisions to convert the Home's chapel into other uses, to give the chapel furnishings and vestments to mission churches, like St. Mary's in Vernonia, Oregon, to eliminate all courses in religion and to separate the Home's identity from the Catholic Church in everything except name.

In his earlier years, Hamilton discreetly wore clerical attire, which was, at least many people thought so, symbolic of the Church's presence. But as time passed, he dropped this form of identity, also. He appeared in secular clothes habitually, more often than not in casual attire. Some of the staff applauded him; others resented the changes.

These matters surfaced occasionally in meetings of the Board of Trustees. During one meeting of both boards, Hamilton was called upon to defend his policies.

> *In answer to Fr. [Frank] Campbell's question about religion, Fr. Hamilton pointed out that religion was not being taught except by model from the staff. He pointed out that most boys leave the campus to return home on weekends and that counselors do, from time to time, take the boys to a folk Mass. Archbishop Power and Fr. Park pursued the matter of moral instruction and values. It was pointed out that at St. Mary's the percentage of Catholics is only 5% and that in such an institution it was found very difficult to effectively teach religion. It was also mentioned that Boys Town is spending considerable monies for researching this problem. It was suggested that there was a factor of Christianity in the staff showing "care" for these boys who have previously been rejected, but there was no true religious emphasis at St. Mary's.*[14]

Dr. Marsh had some good things to say about Hamilton.

"Hamilton," he told me, reflecting quietly on events of long ago, "did a remarkable job in cleaning up [St. Mary's, grounds and buildings]. The building's were refurbished and debris on campus removed. The kids smiled more. A lot of positive things happened. It was a time of [high] level sophistication — made St. Mary's look good. St. Mary's, which was once considered a "dumping ground," by most CSD workers, now wanted to place kids there, even with a long waiting list of six to nine months."

By the early 1980's, Marsh added, "St. Mary's had a treatment room for out-of-control kids. Social workers had been hired to deal with the families of boys. Outside speakers had been brought in to lecture on the state-of-the-art treatment."

In all of this, Emma Dennis had been very supportive. Emma was, in fact, a major element in this stream of progress, as was Dr. Marsh. There seems to be no doubt that Hamilton inherited some remarkable professionals like these two. He had gathered others to form an unbeatable team which gave him opportunities for what might be regarded as "extra curricular activities."

These actions, like running for political office, doubtlessly influenced his relationship to St. Mary's, since they pulled him away from campus involvement. Eventually he resigned as director and left the active ministry of the priesthood as well, confirming in the minds of some their antecedent bias against his goals and style. One cannot judge his motives or his sincerity, but only his record, whatever its limitations, and on the basis of this, Hamilton comes off better than some of his predecessors.

Emma Dennis

William Hamilton departed from St. Mary's during July of 1986. Emma Dennis succeeded him as "Acting Director" at that time. The choice, as the sequel demonstrates, was a very good one.

Emma has enjoyed a long association with St. Mary's, like others on the staff, Mike Cole and Dr. Loyal Marsh. She had considerable experience in administration. It has been suggested, presumably by those who know, that she had really served as "Acting Director" for sometime before this, without office or portfolio. Whatever this, no one could dispute her benign influence. In a brief time she was confirmed in her position with the title of Executive Director, which she retains today.

Emma had been born in the Midwest, in Elgin, North Dakota. Lived on the family farm, south of Raleigh, where people instinctively put important things first.[15] She arrived in Oregon directly from North Dakota, without being exposed to the virus of sunshine-at-any-cost, to which some unfortunate people succumb. Raleigh, a one horse town, was in cattle country, south of Bismark. When Emma reached high school age, she attended a convent boarding school conducted by the School Sisters of Notre Dame. She found a companion there who shared her deep faith and in the course of time, both decided that they wanted to become missionaries. From a book, which presented brief descriptions of each of the American Congregations of Sisters, they selected the Franciscan Missionary Sisters. So, after completing high school, they applied and were accepted eventually by Mother Leola. They arrived at Beaverton in 1959. Emma's companion remained for one year only, then returned to her home in the Midwest.

Fr. Goodrich was Superintendent at that time, and Emma made her novitiate in the convent on the Boys Home grounds, behind the famous enclosure.

"Father Goodrich," she told me, "was a spiritual person with the ability to relate to the public. He had a charismatic personality. His sermons were brilliant and he had a beautiful tenor voice for singing. People came to hear him sing — at Midnight Mass the chapel was crowded to the rafters."

Emma is an intense kind of person but is not impetuous. She reflects carefully before answering questions. "Goodrich," she said finally, "saw the child with his eyes only. Children manipulated him. In classrooms they acted up. He firmly believed that you do not need clinical help — only sacraments would take care of the problem. He was criticized for mandatory Mass attendance."

Like many of the Sisters who joined the Franciscan Missionary Sisters between 1959 and 1962, Emma decided to leave the community. She received her dispensation in January 1970, then remained at St. Mary's as a staff member. It all sounded very simple when she related it, but one knows that she experienced countless frustrations, depression and spiritual suffering during those difficult years of decision and transition. This is one reason why she became a highly qualified professional; she had suffered much, like most of the boys who came to her for help.

Archbishop William Levada

The departure of William Hamilton from St. Mary's coincided with the departure of Archbishop Cornelius Power. On July 1, 1986, Bishop William Levada, Titular Bishop of Capri and Auxiliary Bishop of Los Angeles, was designated publicly as Power's successor in Portland. The new Archbishop was installed on September 2, 1986.

An attractive, courtly prelate, with animated facial features like Archbishop Sheen's, Levada made a dramatic entrance. Not exactly a stranger to the bishop watchers of the West Coast, he was expected to make some tough decisions about the Church in Portland. Like the other dioceses of the country, Portland faced many seemingly insurmountable obstacles, like replacing the aging priests and the declining number of religious, financing parochial schools with fewer practicing Catholics, resolving the abortion impasse and restoring family stability. Stress with problems like these had contributed to burn-out for Bishops like Power and many active priests. Levada did not disappoint his watchers, in or out of the Archdiocese.

Among his first crises was the Boys Home. Father Hamilton departed shortly after his arrival. Some of the older priests had little good to say about it. A few were demanding that it be closed. How,

Most Rev. William J. Levada, S.T.D., Eighth Archbishop of Portland in Oregon (1986 -   ).

they asked righteously, could the Archdiocese prudently sponsor a sex offenders' treatment center which contained less than five percent Catholic boys?

Supporters of St. Mary's could point to Father Flanagan's Boys Town near Omaha. This had become, in fact, a non-denominational institution, which retained its ties to the Archdiocese and preserved the spiritual values of its founder. Certainly, as some pointed out later, "the care for society's homeless — the 'social orphans' who are functionally homeless due to their victimization in abusive families," falls within the Church's pastoral mission.

The Independent Program Assessment

The new Archbishop was willing to hear more. At his request, Father Val Peter, Executive Director of Father Flanagan's Boys Town, arranged for "an independent program assessment" of St. Mary's by members of the Boys Town staff.[16]

Among the reasons given for this assessment, one stood out from the others. "Relatively recent changes in program direction including a special program to serve a sexual offender population." The focus of the project, then, included this controversial subject "as to custodial safety issues and treatment design."

The focus would cover several other sensitive areas, which had been discussed frequently by members of both boards.

1. *Development and clarification of the Advisory Board's role with that of the Board of Trustees.*
2. *St. Mary's relationship with the Archdiocese and integration of the Catholic Church's doctrine into St. Mary's philosophy and mission.*
3. *Evaluation and recommendations concerning the Special Education Program.*
4. *Recommendations concerning the adequacy of the campus facilities.*
5. *Fund raising methods and functions of the Development Office.*[17]

The results of the survey were published in a sixty-one page document by Dr. Daniel Daly and Patricia Leahy. For the most part, this made explicit what many observers already knew. They already knew, for example, that "communication between Board of Trustees/Advisory Board" would receive a less than perfect rating. They already knew that the Home's current relationship with the Archdiocese was a severe handicap in fund raising, that "St. Mary's needs to become more aggressive about raising money," and that St. Mary's "is one of the lower [state] funded programs of its kind," meaning that St. Mary's is more dependent on private sources for money than similar institutions elsewhere.

The report, however, is definitely supportive and contains many positive judgements which confirm the administration and its direction, and also its manner of following it. Significantly, I think, the highest ratings of the Home were submitted by the Referral Agencies. Several comments by respondents deserve to be recorded here.

> "Excellent program — need more like it for emotionally disturbed children."
>
> "St. Mary's has provided the treatment and the commitment to children I have not experienced, even at Boy's Town. Our state has recently ordered no children to be placed out of state so unfortunately St. Mary's can no longer be used. We have no program in Washington State that comes close to the dedicated, practical, professional treatment provided at St. Mary's. Thanks for the opportunity."[18]

A New Spiritual Program

St. Mary's had passed the "Independent Assessment" test with a modicum of dignity. Knowledge of the problems, Emma Dennis already knew, did not make them go away. She was especially touchy about the "secularization" problem, the lack of more spiritual influences on the boys.

"We had the boys fill out a questionnaire on religion," she told me. "We asked questions like these: Did or do you go to church? Did or do your parents or grandparents go to church? Do you believe in a Higher Power? In life after death?

"We received mostly "no's" on all questions. The question is how do we teach kids to behave differently if we don't teach values? To retain the progress achieved when authority figures in their homes are not around? How do we internalize these new behaviors and values? How do we develop a conscience in a child?"

"Prayers are said at mealtimes," the Boys Town report states, "and religious practices (e.g. church attendance) are supported if the residents or their guardians request them."

When the boys, or their parents, requested opportunities to attend Church, arrangements were cheerfully made to bus them to the church of their choice. "Mormons are the best in bringing their children to church," Emma said. "We have a number of kids from Evangelical backgrounds. One of them attends church and sings in the choir. He never misses church on Sunday."

Emma had introduced a multi-denominational religious program, which the Boys Town report noted as follows:

> *In the past year, Emma Dennis has initiated practices that reflect an attitude shift toward more spiritual development activities for youth. For instance, a pastoral counseling practicum has been established for Catholic seminarians. Seminarians ran values clarification groups on campus last summer. These groups were voluntary and not part of the curriculum for each resident, but reports are that they were well received by the youth who participated.*[19]

This experiment has proved to be so effective that St. Mary's acquired a highly qualified "youth minister" to "develop the whole child", an experienced person who had been previously engaged in a catechesis program in Arizona. Attendance at classes is strictly voluntary. "But there is a full house each time." Emma added proudly, "There are fifteen to twenty in the group."

Emma paused to think about it.

Photo courtesy of the *Oregonian*.

Emma Dennis comforting Conrad.

St. Mary's Now

The *Oregonian* in its MetroWest edition of July 6, 1989, presents on its front page a dramatic photograph in full color. The Executive Director of St. Mary's, Emma Dennis, the caption states, shares a quiet moment with Conrad, age 12. Conrad is a handsome black boy with dark eyes and a crown of heavy brown curly hair, and he hugs his large teddy bear and stares into space. The eyes are very sad and only God knows what pain they see.

Beside him, giving him comfort by just being there, Emma, her eyes cast down, stares into space also. Her mouth expresses sorrow, too. As she sits there, her arms around the boy, she is like a grieving madonna. One is reminded of the Pieta, the Sorrowful Mother and the victim of men's malice.

Where would Conrad be without Emma and St. Mary's? It is a frightening thought. Where would the other boys be?

As I wandered around the clipped green campus on a clear sunny day that month of July, I saw there victims of a society in turmoil, mostly attractive boys who need love and understanding, and sometimes a stern rebuke or a harsh warning. None are so cynical or mixed up that he cannot respond to love, which he seldom experienced before. I saw them mowing the lawn, weeding the flower beds and playing games like other boys. Seven out of ten of these boys will find peace and a normal, happy life. The others have been injured beyond repair in this world, but not beyond salvation in the next.

So I saw St. Mary's in a new light. Was this a Calvary where sin is expiated, where sufferings united to that of Jesus "fill up those things that are wanting to the sufferings of Christ." St. Mary's cannot be explained in any other way.

In this the boys of St. Mary's deserve the love and compassion of all of us.

Epilogue

ST. MARY'S ON THE THRESHOLD of a new century, is still engaged in the same struggle as it was in the beginning of the first, the battle between the Spirit of God and the spirit of the world. Time has made it only more complex, and in some respects, more gross. But the elements of poverty, loneliness, willfulness and fear are still there, waiting to be exorcised.

The stage, too, is still there, one half mile from the first one. The complaints are still there. It still rains sometimes, and sometimes a roof leaks. The Sisters come for brief visits, sitting in wheelchairs or clutching canes, still smiling. Former boys, wearing their ages and respectability with honor, return to observe the young boys, and to reminisce. They see that much has changed, but not so much they cannot recognize their former lodgings. Some changes, they say, are for the better. Nothing is perfect. One learns this as he grows older. Seeing the bright side, they know from experience that St. Mary's Home for Boys, whatever its priorities are now, is still a success.

Notes

Chapter 1

1. Mother Joseph's statue was accepted by Congress and placed in the National Hall of Fame. It was formally dedicated on May 1, 1980. Cf. Schoenberg, Wilfred P., S.J., *A History of The Catholic Church In The Pacific Northwest 1743-1983*, Washington, 1987, p. 737.

2. Archives of the Sisters of the Holy Names, Marylhurst, Oregon, hereafter referred to as SNJMA, *Chronicle*, Villa Marie, Oregon, Introduction, 1908.

3. This reference on site, appears to be in error. The school was on Fifth and Mill, according to Sister Rosemarie Kasper, S.N.J.M., archivist.

4. *Ibid.*

5. SNJMA, *Chronicle*, St. Mary's Academy for dates as presented.

6. *Ibid.*

7. *Catholic Sentinel*, January 4, 1880. The early land titles are very complex. Both Adam Heineman and I spent many hours in the records in the Washington County Courthouse at Hillsboro. Adam had better connections than I, and produced many more documents.

8. Much has been published about this famous Archbishop's death. The best work is: Steckler, Gerard G., S.J., *Charles John Seghers Priest and Bishop In The Pacific Northwest 1839-1886: A Biography*, Fairfield, (Wash.), 1986.

9. Gross was happy in Savannah and regarded his appointment to Oregon City as a come down to poverty and the wilderness. He soon changed his mind.

10. The Vicariate was raised to the status of the Diocese of Boise on August 26, 1893.

11. Schoenberg, Wilfred P., S.J., *These Valiant Women*, Beaverton, (Oregon), 1986, p. 98.

12. Archives of the Sisters of St. Mary of Oregon, Beaverton, hereafter cited as SSMOA, manuscript, "Memoirs of Mother Wilhelmina," p. 33.

13. One of the Sisters, Mary Afra, the blind one, was left behind, because the others had no place to care for her. She died a short time later. One other had been spirited away and placed with a Catholic family, because her father threatened to restrain her. She joined the Sisters at Maria Zell.

14. The Catholics at Sublimity had requested a priest from Archbishop Blanchet in June 1877. Father Peter Stampfl, the first resident priest, arrived on December 3, 1879.

15. *Catholic Sentinel,* January 4, 1880.

16 *Ibid.,* May 9, 1889, noted that the Hornbuckle property blocked access, and that the corridor had been acquired.

17. *Ibid.,* February 7, 1889.

18. Archives of the Fathers of the Most Precious Blood, Carthagena, Ohio, personnel record for Alphone Grassi.

19. SSMOA, manuscript, Sister Mary Pulcheria Sparkman, "And So It Happened and Not By Chance," p. 101.

Chapter 2

1. This text and a portion of the following, has been taken verbatim from Schoenberg, Wilfred P., S.J., *These Valiant Women,* Beaverton (Oregon), 1986, with the permission of Sister Anna Hertel, S.S.M.O., Superior General of the Sisters of St. Mary of Oregon.

2. SSMOA, Accounts for St. Mary's Home, Volume 1.

3. Snider, Sister Mary Celestine, S.S.M.O., "The Dawn," Master of Arts Thesis, University of Portland, [1944], p. 72.

4. *Ibid.,* p. 80.

5. SSMOA, manuscript, "Reminiscence of Lawrence Farnsworth," *passim.*

6. Joseph Schell and John Heinrich carried a longtime feud in public against Christie, allegedly for an injustice. Cf. Schoenberg, Wilfred P., S.J., *A History of The Catholic Church In The Pacific Northwest 1743-1983,* Washington, 1987, p. 423 *et seq.,* and p. 431 *et seq.*

Chapter 3

1. SSMOA, St. Mary's Boys Home, Letter of Gross to Mother Seraphim, June 23, 1896.

2. SSMOA, manuscript, Sister M. Frances Zenner, S.S.M.O., archivist, "Class Notes History of the Community of St. Mary's of Oregon," p. 6.

3. Most priests in the Portland area, favored the suggestion that the Sisters of St. Mary be required to join another previously existing community.

4. This was the former home of Vicar General Bartholomew Delorme, "A well furnished roomy building." *Catholic Sentinel,* July 2, 1908.

5. SNJMA, manuscript, "Historical Sketches of the History of Christie School."

6. Heesacker, Father Joseph, quoted in [Eberhard, Sister Mary Eugenia, S.S.M.O.], *Souvenir of Golden Jubilee, 1886-1936,* (Beaverton), 1936, p. 46.

7. SSMOA, manuscript, "Reminiscences of Lawrence Farnsworth," p. 40.

8. Moore died on January 29, 1907.

9. This figure given by Maxwell is inaccurate. Only 58 acres were acquired to fill in a corner of the original property.

10. Held's Technical College on Spokane's south side, burned to the ground just after it was occupied in October 1897. It was never reopened.

11. In Deeney's tenure, the parish was called St. Mary's.

12. Heesacker, *op. cit.*, p. 47.

13. The cemetery, located at that time on the Sisters' ten acres, was moved to the new motherhouse grounds in 1970.

Chapter 4

1. Heesacker, Father Joseph, quoted in [Eberhard, Sister Mary Eugenia, S.S.M.O.], *Souvenir of Golden Jubilee 1886-1936,* (Beaverton), 1936, p. 47.

2. Emma H. Anderson, wife of Levi, deceased, died on September 25, 1904, having bequeathed to the Archdiocese her estate valued at $75,049.20. Terms of this bequest were so complex that problems related to it continued to surface for years to come.

3. Archives of the Archdiocese of Portland in Oregon, hereafter cited as AAP, correspondence regarding St. Mary's Boys Home, February 19, 1979. The documents related to this are in Washington County Courthouse, Hillsboro, Vol. 116, p. 395-397.

4. Heesacker, *op. cit.*

5. SSMOA, Jacques, Sister Mary Christina, S.S.M.O., manuscript, "Memoirs Of St. Mary's Home For Boys," p. 122.

6. *Catholic Sentinel,* July 31, 1930.

7. Archives of St. Mary's Boys Home, herein after referred to as ASM, manuscript, "Data About St. Mary's Home."

8. ASM, manuscript, Father James Maxwell, "St. Mary's Boys Home," 1939.

9. ASM, manuscript, "Data About St. Mary's Home."

10. This and following incidents are described by Sister Mary Christina in her manuscript memoirs cited above.

Chapter 5

1. SSMOA, Poster, "St. Mary's," [c. 1943].

2. SSMOA, manuscript, Jacques, Sister Mary Christina, S.S.M.O., "Memoirs of St. Mary's Home For Boys," p. 118.

3. Hansen, Richard, manuscript, "Memories of St. Mary's Home for Boys — 1938 to 1941," Copy in Oregon Province Archives, Spokane, hereafter cited as OPA.

4. This and some selections following have been taken verbatim from, Schoenberg, Wilfred P., S.J., *These Valiant Women,* Beaverton (Oregon), 1986, with the permission of Sister Anna Hertel, S.S.M.O., Superior General of the Sisters of St. Mary of Oregon.

5. ASM, Minutes of the Advisory Board Meeting, November 17, 1950.

Chapter 6

1. A detailed and lively account of this appears in Pottebaum, Rev. Mother M. Leola, O.S.F., *Strange Paths,* an unpublished manuscript in the Archives of the Franciscan Missionary Sisters, hereafter cited as AFMS.

2. AFMS, manuscript, Fan, Rev. Anthony Kuo, [Former Student of], "The Sketches About The Life of Bishop Raphael Palazzi," p. 4.

3. AFMS, manuscript, [Palazzi, Bishop Raphael], "An Historical Summary and Chronological Report of the New Congregation of the Franciscan Missionary Sisters of the Adolorata."

4. These and subsequent data appear in Pottebaum, *Strange Paths, passim.*

5. AFMS, letter [Pottebaum] to Father Terrence Cronin, O.F.M., September 5, 1961. This contains a brief history of the congregation. Its contents reveal authorship.

6. Bishop Aloysius Joseph Willinger resigned on October 25, 1967 and died on July 25, 1973.

7. AFMS, unsigned manuscript, "Prologue," an account of Bishop Raphael Palazzi, O.F.M. and the Franciscan Missionary Sisters.

8. AFMS, Sister Angela Merici, OSF, and Mrs. Grace Coppernoll, unpublished manuscript history of the Franciscan Missionary Sisters, Chapter 24, p. 2.

9. AFMS, Copy of agreement between the Archdiocese of Portland in Oregon and The Franciscan Sisters of Our Sorrowful Mother. [Franciscan Missionary Sisters].

10. ASM, Minutes of Advisory Board Meeting in March, 1953.

11. AFMS, Letter of Goodrich to Mother Leola, March 20, 1953.

12. AFMS, Letter of Mother Leola to Goodrich, April 12, 1953.

13. AFMS, Letter of Mother Leola to Goodrich, May 16, 1953.

14. AFMS, Merici and Coppernoll, unpublished manuscript history, Chapter 24, p. 23 *et seq.*

15. AFMS, Transcriptions: Sisters Angela Merici and Dolores [Special Account #26-105], "Oregon Miscellaneous," p. 1.

16. AFMS, A letter from Sister Angela Merici [Special Account #26-92], Thanksgiving Day, 1953, p. 2 *et seq.*

Chapter 7

1. This has been confirmed by a member of the board, who stated that "Goodrich had money in seventeen banks."
2. ASM, Minutes of Advisory Board Meeting on May 9, 1952.
3. This total adds up to 160, the number of all the boys in residence during the year. Another report gives admissions at 104, with 103 at the end of 1955.
4. AFMS, Report on Children served at St. Mary's in 1955.
5. This system came into use about 1958. Cf. ASM, Fact Sheet for 1964.
6. ASM, Letter of Dahl to Goodrich, April 21, 1958.
7. The Craft Shop was built by the Knights of Columbus of Oregon in 1957.
8. *St. Mary's Chimes,* April, 1963.
9. ASM, Minutes of Advisory Board Meeting on December 11, 1958.
10. *Ibid.,* October 10, 1960.
11. *Ibid,* December 20, 1960.
12. ASM, "Fact Sheet" for 1963.
13. Lockup, reportedly practiced by police authorities, meant what it says, boys locked in jail until they calmed down.
14. AFMS, Sister's Work Schedule (Weekly) St. Mary's Home for Boys, 1966-1967.
15. ASM, Minutes of the Advisory Board, September 26, 1963.
16. *Ibid.,* May 16, 1963. An elaborate plan with options had been worked out by Goodrich and staff.
17. AFMS, Memorandum regarding conditions for Sisters' Continuance at St. Mary's, c. 1966.
18. AFMS, Letter of Seven Franciscan Missionary Sisters at St. Mary's Boys Home to McCoy, September 3, 1966.
19. ASM, Program description of functions, including description of program and plans, p. 5.
20. ASM, special written report of Goodrich to the Advisory Board Members, February, 1967.

Chapter 8

1. Interview with Marsh, August 15, 1989.
2. AFMS, letter of Sister Raymond to Sister Mary Ancilla, November 15, 1967.
3. Beaverton's *Valley Times,* September 26, 1968.
4. Interview with Warren, August 6, 1989.
5. Interview with Marsh, August 15, 1989.
6. ASM, Minutes of Advisory Board Meeting, February 18, 1970.
7. Interview with Boyle, August 6, 1989.

8. The Motherhouse was moved to Santa Cruz in 1967. It was moved back to Beaverton in 1986.

9. Interview with Marsh, August 15, 1989.

10. ASM, Minutes of Advisory Board Meeting, April 5, 1969.

11. *Catholic Sentinel,* April 10, 1969.

12. ASM, Minutes of Advisory Board Meeting, July 14, 1970.

13. Under Boyle, the number of resident boys, usually referred to as "population," ran a bit higher than 40 at one time. Later averages were higher.

14. ASM, Minutes of Annual Meeting of Trustees, July 14, 1970.

15. *Journal,* October 6, 1969.

16. ASM, Report on Jesuit Novitiate, February 24, 1970.

17. ASM, Minutes of Advisory Board Meeting, February 18, 1970.

18. ASM, Park report to Trustees, January 24, 1970. Actual cost for 1970 was $276,325. For 1971 it was $299,187.

19. ASM, Boyle to Merici, March 25, 1970.

20. ASM, Minutes of Advisory Board Meeting, July 14, 1970.

21. A photograph of the collapsing building appears in *Valley Times* for July 30, 1970.

22. ASM, Minutes of Board of Trustees, March 5, 1971.

23. AFMS, Letter of McQuarry to Sister Raymond, November 18, 1971.

24. AFMS, Letter of Boyle to Sister Angela, April 28, 1969.

25. AFMS, Financial Statement, St. Mary's Home For Boys, Sister Mary Dolores, 1969-1973.

26. AFMS, *Newsletter,* March, 1972.

27. *Ibid.*

28. *Valley Times,* July 27, 1972.

29. AFMS, *Newsletter,* March, 1972.

30. ASM, Letter of Hamilton to Sister Angela, February 21, 1974.

31. AFMS, Minutes of Cabinet Meeting, Santa Cruz, March 2, 1974.

32. AFMS, Minutes of Cabinet Meeting, Santa Cruz, March 16, 1974.

Chapter 9

1. Archbishop Dwyer's resignation was accepted on January 22, 1974.

2. ASM, Hamilton to Power, September 2, 1974.

3. *Ibid.,* February 2, 1977.

4. ASM, Report on Senior Staff meeting for September 1977.

5. ASM, Minutes of Advisory Board Meeting, November 3, 1977.

6. *Valley Times,* August 11, 1979.

7. Archbishop Howard was born on November 5, 1877.

8. The reunions have been held every two years since 1978. A special reunion for the Centennial Year was held on August 20, 1989.

9. ASM, these excerpts from Minutes of the Advisory Board on date given.

10. *Catholic Sentinel,* May 8, 1981.

11. ASM, Minutes of Advisory Board Meeting, October 6, 1982.

12. *The St. Mary's Times,* Vol. I., No. 1 (April 1989). A new in-house periodical.

13. Marsh, Dr. Loyal, Ph.D., Patrick Connell, M.S. and Ellen Olson,B.A., *Breaking The Cycle Adolescent Sexual Treatment Manual,* Beaverton (Oregon), 1988, p. 12.

14. ASM, Minutes of Joint Meeting of Both Boards, December 2, 1972.

15. Interview with Marsh, July 24, 1989.

16. ASM, Program of Assessment of St. Mary's Home For Boys, May 11-13, 1988, Prepared by the Boys Town National Family Home Program, Daniel L. Daly, Ph.D., Patricia A. Leahy.

17. The numbering of these items is mine.

18. *Ibid.*

19. These were Seminarians from Mount Angel.